# INFLATION

*by Steve Forbes & Elizabeth Ames*

*Reviving America: How Repealing Obamacare, Replacing the Tax Code
and Reforming The Fed will Restore Hope and Prosperity*

*MONEY: How the Destruction of the Dollar Threatens the
Global Economy—and What We Can Do About It*

*Freedom Manifesto: Why Free Markets Are Moral
and Big Government Isn't*

*How Capitalism Will Save Us: Why Free People and Free Markets
Are the Best Answer in Today's Economy*

*by Steve Forbes*

*Flat Tax Revolution: Using a Postcard to Abolish the IRS*

*A New Birth of Freedom: Vision for America*

*Power Ambition Glory: The Stunning Parallels Between Great Leaders
of the Ancient World and Today . . . and the Lessons You Can Learn*
(and John Prevas)

*by Nathan Lewis*

*Gold: The Once and Future Money*

*Gold: The Monetary Polaris*

*Gold: The Final Standard*

*The Magic Formula: The Timeless Secret to
Economic Health and Prosperity*

STEVE FORBES
NATHAN LEWIS
ELIZABETH AMES

# INFLATION

WHAT IT IS, WHY IT'S BAD,
AND HOW TO FIX IT

ENCOUNTER BOOKS  NEW YORK · LONDON

First American edition published in 2022 by Encounter Books, an activity of Encounter for Culture and Education, Inc., a nonprofit, tax-exempt corporation.
Encounter Books website address: www.encounterbooks.com

Manufactured in the United States and printed on acid-free paper. The paper used in this publication meets the minimum requirements of ANSI/NISO Z39.48—1992 (R 1997) (*Permanence of Paper*).

Infographic on p. 35 by ILMDesigns.com

Image on p. 122 is from Wikimedia Commons, DonkeyHotey, licensed under CC by 2.0. It was originally adapted from the Statue of Liberty Coin designed by Don Everhart from the Presidential Coin Series at the US Mint and converted to grayscale for the purposes of this book. https://creativecommons.org/licenses/by/2.0/deed.en

FIRST AMERICAN EDITION

LIBRARY OF CONGRESS CATALOGING-IN-PUBLICATION DATA

Names: Forbes, Steve, 1947- author. | Lewis, Nathan K., 1971- author. | Ames, Elizabeth, 1954- author.
Title: Inflation: what it is, why it's bad, and how to fix it / by Steve Forbes, Nathan Lewis, and Elizabeth Ames.
Description: New York, NY : Encounter Books, [2022]
Includes bibliographical references and index.
Identifiers: LCCN 2021056768 (print) | LCCN 2021056769 (ebook)
ISBN 9781641772433 (hardcover) | ISBN 9781641772440 (ebook)
Subjects: LCSH: Inflation (Finance) | Money.
Classification: LCC HG229 .F644 2022  (print) | LCC HG229  (ebook) | DDC 332.4/1—dc23/eng/20211209
LC record available at https://lccn.loc.gov/2021056768
LC ebook record available at https://lccn.loc.gov/2021056769

1 2 3 4 5 6 7 8 9 20 22

*This book is dedicated to people
around the world who have endured
the hardships of inflation,
and who want something better.*

# Contents

# Introduction

I*NFLATION*. The headlines are everywhere: "Fears of High Inflation Getting Worse?"; "Consumer Prices Jump;" "Inflation Marks Quickest Pace in More Than a Decade."

The front page of the *New York Post* proclaims that producer prices have skyrocketed and inflation is the worst it has been in years.

A shopper at a Long Island supermarket complains that his grocery bill has doubled in just two months. He's now buying only essentials, skipping pricier items like meat and fish.

A Virginia car dealer marvels that prices are moving up so fast that "some common, used cars are selling at more than their original sticker price when they were new."

A realtor in South Carolina complains that the high cost of lumber is impeding construction of new homes, driving housing prices out of sight.

Bloomberg News reports that customers of a bike store in California are aghast to discover that the price of a top-of-the-line mountain bike jumped 10 percent in less than six months to nearly $4,800. The price tag on future models is expected to go still higher.

Almost daily, people are shocked by media reports of double-digit increases in the price of food, gas, automobiles, and other essentials. Adding to public anxiety is an ever-mounting level of government spending, causing federal debt to now exceed the size of the entire US economy. Much of this massive obligation is being financed by the Federal Reserve, the US central bank, through Treasury bonds that it pays for with money it created out of thin air.

This aggressive spending, combined with the Fed's money creation, has unleashed an ocean of dollars into the economy. Between December 2019 and mid-2021, the money supply exploded by more than 35 percent, exceeding an astonishing $20 *trillion*.

Alarms have been sounding about the potential of so much "money printing" to create a dangerous inflation. Among the first to voice concerns was Larry Summers, the Keynesian economist who served as treasury secretary during the Clinton administration, and later as chief economic advisor to President Obama. He openly worried that "we're taking very substantial risks on the inflation side." Summers went on to warn: "We are printing money, we are creating government bonds, we are borrowing on unprecedented scales. Those are things that surely create more of a risk of a sharp dollar decline than we had before. And sharp dollar declines are much more likely to translate themselves into inflation than they were historically."

Summers and others fear a replay of the "Great Inflation" of the 1970s, when the US endured a decade of double-digit price increases combined with a stagnant economy. The word "stagflation"—used during that era to describe the malaise—has made a comeback in public discussions. Some observers even raise the specter of a hyperinflation comparable to the historic crisis that ravaged Weimar Germany in the early 1920s and the maelstroms currently tearing apart Venezuela and other nations today.

However, officials at the Federal Reserve initially dismissed such warnings. They insisted the price increases were "transitory"—the effect of COVID supply-chain disruptions. Yet, by the end of the year, their tune began to change. With inflation blowing past 6 percent, Federal Reserve Chair Jerome Powell conceded that it was likely "a good time to 'retire' that word."

President Joe Biden, for his part, has shrugged off concerns about the price hikes and all that government spending. Echoing an increasingly popular, far-left view known as "Modern Monetary Theory," he has insisted that government spending actually *suppresses* inflation. How does it do this? Biden explained in a 2021 White House speech that it "breaks up the bottlenecks in our economy."

The president raised eyebrows even among Keynesian economists (ordinarily proponents of central-bank monetary "stimulus") when he went on to add that massive spending on infrastructure

> will enhance our productivity—raising wages without raising prices. That won't increase inflation. It will take the pressure off of inflation, give a boost to our workforce, which leads to lower prices in the years ahead.

*Really?* Events are still playing out. But one thing is certain: confusion reigns when it comes to inflation. From the fall of Rome to the housing bust and global financial crisis of 2008, the misunderstanding of money has led to countless disasters that have disordered lives and societies. Much of the destruction could have been avoided if more people had understood the causes and consequences of inflation.

This book is a plainspoken discussion of why inflation happens, and why, contrary to the insistence of so many in Washington, DC, almost any level of inflation is "bad" for both the economy and for society.

As we observe in Chapter One, misconceptions about inflation are nearly as abundant as Zimbabwe dollars. (Zimbabwe is one of the great inflaters of all time.) We're often told, for example, that the Fed needs to create "a little inflation" to boost employment and create prosperity. Yet, when there is "too much" prosperity, we hear that the central bank needs to raise interest rates to *prevent* inflation by keeping the economy from "overheating." The contradictions can make one's head spin.

Even those who are concerned—with good reason—about today's gargantuan government spending often don't get it right. You'll often hear fears that a ballooning federal debt "will be paid for by future generations." The reality is that we're paying for it already through the stealth tax of inflation.

These misguided perceptions have consistently yielded inaccurate inflation forecasts. In late 2020, Fed officials predicted a minimal level of only 1.8 percent inflation for the following year, according to the Personal Consumption Expenditures index (PCE), their preferred yardstick. Dream on. By late 2021, the PCE had shot past 5 percent—and inflation accounted for *74 percent* of nominal GDP growth.

Such bad forecasts, too often, produce bad policies. No

surprise, most inflation remedies devised by "experts" most often fail and usually worsen the malaise. This is true not only of chronic hyperinflaters like Venezuela, but also of developed countries including the US.

The most notorious example of a failed remedy was the "Nixon Shock," imposed by President Richard Nixon in 1971. This misguided response consisted of wage and price controls, tariffs, and, worst of all, abandonment of the Bretton Woods gold standard. By severing the link to gold, it turned the once rock-solid dollar—the foundation of America's prosperity—into unstable "fiat money" that fluctuated on world currency markets.

Nixon's "Shock" plunged the world financial system into chaos. It ushered in the "Great Inflation" of the 1970s, the energy crisis, and five decades of monetary instability. We are still feeling the effects today. They include not just the 2021 inflation, but also the financial crisis of 2008-09, and a long-term erosion of the US dollar, whose value, as defined by the price of gold, has dropped by 98 percent.

Like other calamitous "remedies" described in this book, Nixon's "cure" failed because it exacerbated the fundamental cause of inflation. That is, a decline in the value of currency—in this case, the dollar.

Since the invention of currency, all too many leaders have failed to understand that money, first and foremost, is a measure of worth. To fulfill this role, and for markets to function, its value must be stable. The 4,000-year history of money amounts to a repeated pattern where governments attempt to solve their various problems by altering their currency, typically decreasing its value. The effects of this are so bad that subsequent governments vow never to repeat these mistakes. Yet somehow, they always do.

The great physicist Isaac Newton was among those who understood that stable money was as fundamental a concept as his venerated Law of Gravity. As head of the British Royal Mint, Newton, with the help of his friend, the philosopher John Locke, reformed the coinage in the 1690s, making it more uniform and keeping its value unchanged. Later, in 1717, Newton fixed the value of the British pound to gold at three pounds, seventeen shillings, and ten-and-a-half pence (or £3.89) an ounce, a ratio that held for more than 200 years.

Britain's commitment to unchanging, gold-based money formed the foundation for the country's rising wealth and its emergence as a global financial center. Toward the end of the eighteenth century, it became the birthplace of the Industrial Revolution. The reliable British pound helped turn that small island from a second-tier nation to the mightiest industrial power in the world.

More than seventy years after Newton fixed the pound to the price of gold, Alexander Hamilton established a financial system for the young United States that emulated Britain's example by pegging the dollar to gold and silver. The sound dollar became the linchpin of an historic boom that propelled the young republic to its leadership position in the world's economy. By the late nineteenth century, other European nations, as well as Japan, followed Britain and the US in adopting gold-based currencies. The era of the classical gold standard saw an explosion of trade and innovation that, in many respects, remains unequaled.

In contrast, today's political and economic establishment continues to cling to the idea that "monetary expansion" to create "a little inflation" is necessary to "stimulate the economy." Over time, these attitudes have led to a continuing decline in currency values. The ultimate lesson of history—and of this book—is that no nation has ever gotten rich by eroding the value of its money.

Adam Smith observed centuries ago that true wealth is created by people meeting each other's needs in the marketplace. Buying, selling, and innovating. That is as true today as it was during his time. Wealth is created by technological advances that create jobs, increase productivity, and give rise to still more innovation and wealth creation. Think of the millions of jobs, the countless ancillary businesses, and the spectacular wealth created by devices like the iPhone, for example, or by e-commerce sites like Amazon.com. These innovative businesses, and others like them, are what move humanity forward.

When a currency loses value, certain people may reap windfalls. But society as a whole loses. Inflation's gross distortions of prices and markets stifle growth and advancement, creating unfairness, exacerbating inequality, and inflaming tensions that can lead to social and cultural unraveling—a phenomenon that has been referred to as "The Great Disorder."

Chapter One, "What is Inflation?" explains the difference between what inflation actually is, and what many of us *think* it is. Most people think of inflation as being about "price increases." However, higher prices are the *effect* of inflation, not the cause.

There are actually two types of inflation. The price increases of "non-monetary" inflation are driven by rising demand for products and services that, most often, occurs naturally in markets. The other type is "monetary" inflation, resulting from central bank money printing or other events that cause currencies to lose value. Our focus in this book is on this second type of inflation and how it's been responsible for centuries of economic and social destruction.

Chapter Two, "Not-So-Great Moments in Inflation History," looks at some of the most infamous examples of monetary inflation, beginning with the fall of Rome. All have been "human-caused disasters" brought about by governments debasing their currencies, usually by creating too much money.

However, Chapter Two makes the under-appreciated point that a large money supply does not automatically mean inflation. The value of currency, like the value of everything else in the economy, is determined by the ratio of supply to demand. Thus, tiny Switzerland has little inflation despite having a large money supply relative to its size. That's because the Swiss franc is in high demand as one of the world's most trusted currencies.

Chapter Two also looks at the question being asked today by socialist advocates of Modern Monetary Theory (MMT): *Why can't we just print money?* After all, until the recent pandemic-related price increases, there had been relatively little inflation despite the Fed's historic expansion of the money supply known as "Quantitative Easing," undertaken to revive the economy after the 2008 financial crisis. Proponents of MMT argue, with some justification, that both the Fed and the European Central Bank are already operating according to MMT principles. We explain why this apparent defiance of monetary "gravity" is essentially an anomaly—the result of banking regulations and central-bank maneuvers. These one-time events have hindered bank lending and have kept money from flooding the economy.

More recently, some Fed watchers suspect that a more severe inflation has been held at bay by an arcane-sounding central bank transaction known as a reverse repurchase agreement (informally known as a "reverse repo"). We explain in Chapter Two that this gimmick has been employed by the Fed to mitigate, at least temporarily, the full effects of central bank money creation. It may seem like the Fed can "just print money." But, as rising consumer prices may finally be telling us, gravity can only be defied for so long. The principles of Modern Monetary Theory are a recipe for hyperinflation.

Chapter Three, "Why Inflation Is Bad," explains why *all* degrees of monetary inflation are ultimately destructive. Economists at the Federal Reserve insist that creating a low level of inflation is "good" because they say it encourages prosperity. This misguided belief has become the Fed's Holy Writ, thanks to the influence of the Phillips Curve which supposedly correlates inflation with periods of high employment. Seven Nobel prizes have been awarded to economists who have disproved this misguided association. Yet, like so many bad ideas, it manages to persist. The reality, however, is the reverse. Inflation may initially bring on a "sugar high." But sooner rather than later, the economy and job creation stall.

This is true not only of countries that are the worst monetary offenders. The United States has also paid a price over the last five decades as a result of its slowly weakening dollar. Had the nation maintained its growth rates of the gold-standard years during the 1950s and '60s, it's estimated that the economy would be at least 50 percent bigger than it is today.

But the most devastating effect of inflation is its impact on social trust. Money, after all, was invented to enable trade between strangers by providing a mutually agreed-upon unit of value. In other words, it is a facilitator of trust. Markets are people. When money is no longer a reliable unit of value, not only trade but social relationships ultimately unravel. Nations afflicted by extreme inflation end up experiencing higher levels of crime, corruption, and social unrest. As we have seen throughout history, the end result can be a tragic turn to strongmen and dictators.

This does not have to happen. Chapter Four, "How to End the Malaise," explains that inflation can be stopped surprisingly quickly if properly understood. The problem with inflation-fighting approaches like price controls is that they focus on symptoms of inflation, not the cause, which is a decline in the value of currency. The chapter explores the relatively rare record of inflation-fighting successes: Ludwig Erhard's triumph over Germany's post-World War II inflation; Detroit banker Joseph Dodge's similar victory over inflation in postwar Japan; and Paul Volcker's eventual beating of stagflation in the 1970s in the US. All three succeeded through initiatives aimed at achieving what our co-author Nathan Lewis calls "The Magic Formula"—stable money and lower taxes. This powerful combination has, time and again, rescued sliding currencies and tamed inflation by unleashing vibrant, growing economies with an appetite for money.

The chapter also explores the best way to end today's inflation—a return to gold-based money. The book outlines a proposal for a new gold standard that would stabilize the dollar without requiring that the country maintain a gigantic supply of gold. This system could be implemented in a relatively short time, restoring a sound and stable dollar that would serve as the engine for a new era of entrepreneurial creativity and progress.

Chapter Five, "What About Your Money?" offers guidelines for investing during inflationary times. The chapter makes the seldom-mentioned observation that securities markets are subject to the distortions of inflation. Frothy markets can mask declining values. So, investors need to beware. The conventional wisdom has been that a "balanced" investment portfolio with the best ratio between risk and return is "60/40," meaning 60 percent stocks and 40 percent bonds. Inflation turns this logic on its head. The chapter surveys the basics of inflation investing. We look at the pros and cons of the full range of options, from commodities and Treasury inflation-protected securities (TIPS) to alternative investments like cryptocurrencies.

Chapter Six, "The Way Forward," contains ten "takeaways" that crystallize the key points in this book. It poses the question "Where do we go from here?" That depends whether Americans reawaken to the financial Law of Gravity imparted to us by John Locke and Isaac Newton; namely, the importance of sound money and the destructiveness of inflation.

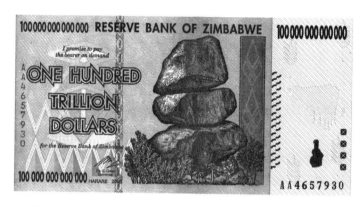

*Zimbabwe's $100 trillion banknote from 2008, an inflation icon.*

## CHAPTER ONE

# What Is Inflation?

T HE NATION of Zimbabwe is one of the world's most notorious inflaters. At one point its hyperinflation got so
bad that the government issued a $100 *trillion* note. Eventu-
ally the country had to throw out its currency and start over,
which they've done more than once. Misconceptions about
inflation may not *literally* outnumber Zimbabwe dollars or,
for that matter, Venezuelan bolívars, or Argentine pesos
(two other hyperinflated currencies). But sometimes it can
seem that way.

Throughout history, inflation has been blamed on everything from bad weather, to unions, to Wall Street greed. In the
early 1920s, Germans blamed the Weimar Republic's infamous
hyperinflation on Jewish shopkeepers and bankers. Centuries
earlier, the ancient Romans blamed theirs on Christians. In
medieval times, inflation was blamed on witches.

Discussions of the subject are rife with fallacies and mis-
taken assumptions. Consumer price increases, for example,

do not automatically signal inflation. Even the much-used description of inflation as coming from "too much money chasing too few goods" can be misleading. While inflation can bring on a soaring cost of living, it can also occur quietly without dramatic increases in consumer prices.

The broad lack of understanding is the reason why policy-makers too often resort to misguided "solutions." In the early 1970s, President Richard Nixon blamed a mild inflation on "international speculators" who, he insisted, were driving down the value of the dollar. His response was the infamous Nixon Shock: a series of initiatives featuring wage and price controls, along with tariffs on imports. Most notoriously, it ended up destroying the Bretton Woods monetary system under which the dollar had had a fixed and stable value defined by an ounce of gold.

The measures were supposed to be temporary. But Nixon's "cure" set in motion the decade-long Great Inflation and the energy crisis of the 1970s, not to mention Nixon's impeachment proceedings and eventual resignation.

We will see later on that the Nixon Shock was typical of most so-called inflation remedies, which more often than not end up making things worse. Their damage to the economy, as well as society, can be lasting.

That was especially true of Nixon's destruction of the Bretton Woods monetary system, which ended the US dollar's long history on the gold standard, the monetary principle that the US had embraced practically since its founding. For nearly 180 years, with only a few interruptions, the value of the dollar was linked to gold. The United States rarely had a problem with inflation and became the most economically successful country in the world.

## A Slowly Eroding Dollar

The end of the Bretton Woods gold standard gave us what we have today: a monetary world order where all currencies, including the dollar, are floating "fiat money." Their values are no longer set, but depend on the whims of currency traders and the policies of central bankers.

This chaotic system has been in place for barely five decades. However, it is rarely questioned and today is considered the norm. People too young to recall anything else do not perceive the destruction it has wreaked. That includes, for starters, the devastating inflation of the 1970s, followed by a gradual, low-grade inflation that began in the mid-1980s. Since 1970, the dollar's purchasing power has been reduced by 86 percent, according to a calculator from the Bureau of Labor Statistics, based on its official cost-of-living measure, the Consumer Price Index (CPI).

Critics, however, point out the index, which doesn't measure certain expenses (most notably, the cost of health insurance) understates the true effects of inflation. The dollar's decline is even more dramatic if we look at the price of gold, the traditional measure of currency value. In 1970, it took $35 to buy an ounce of gold. Today, it takes around $1,800—a 98 percent drop in value.

Oil is another inflation indicator. In the 1960s, oil cost $3 a barrel and oil companies were profitable. By mid-2021, oil cost $75 a barrel, and oil companies could barely get by. (In 2019, many were at risk of defaulting on their debt.) What does this tell us? Oil is certainly not twenty-five times more valuable than it was in 1965. At least until the recent inflation, gasoline has remained cheap enough to enable automakers to churn out big, powerful, luxurious, gas-guzzlers. What the price increase reflects is a sixty-year slide in the value of the dollar.

Two more examples: a Coke and a McDonald's Big Mac. Back in 1970, a 12-ounce can of Coke cost a dime. A Big Mac cost just 65 cents. Fifty years later, the price of the burger has increased nearly eightfold—to around $4.95. You'd be lucky to get the soda in a vending machine for a dollar. Obviously, these products haven't changed. So why the hefty cost increases? The reason: a shrinking dollar.

The dollar's steady, inflationary decline is one reason that people just starting out today often wonder why they can barely make the rent when, years ago, their parents, who made far less money, could afford to buy a house. The primary reason is inflation. Yes, your parents may have earned fewer dollars. But those dollars were worth much more.

## What Inflation Is Versus What People *Think* It Is

So, what exactly is inflation? The word, as used today by the media and in conversation, has a number of different meanings.

**"A Dramatic Change in the CPI."** The cost of living, or Consumer Price Index (CPI), is produced by the US Bureau of Labor Statistics and tracks the cost of living based on the prices of assorted goods and services, along with energy and housing costs. Some people say there's inflation when the CPI shows a sufficient rise in prices to suggest a decline in the purchasing power of the dollar.

Economists and the media first became concerned about

"inflation" in the spring of 2021 when the CPI recorded an increase of 5 percent over the previous year. It was the biggest jump in more than a decade, beyond the annual 2 percent rise that the Fed's economists believe constitutes monetary "stability." (Actually, pushing up prices by 2 percent each year is hardly *stability*. But more on this later.)

**"Price Increases Over Time."** According to the Federal Reserve, "*Inflation occurs when the price of goods and services increases over time.*" The Fed claims that it can occur when demand exceeds supply (what it calls "demand-pull inflation"). Or, it can happen when the cost of supplies increases ("cost-push inflation").

**A Consequence of "Class Struggle?"** Or, how about this take on the subject from the authors of the socialist textbook *Macroeconomics*: "Conflict theory situates the problem of inflation as being intrinsic to the power relations between workers and capital (class conflict), which are mediated by government within a capitalist system."

Let's just say that last one's a bit too far out to address. As for the other definitions, they may score points for clarity. Yet they, too, are off the mark. Why? Because they focus on increasing prices, which are only the symptoms, and not the cause of inflation.

**The Truth About Prices.** Defining an inflationary malaise simply as "rising prices" does not really describe what is taking place. Economists love to talk about the need for "price stability" in a healthy economy. That idea is fallacious. In a normal economy, prices rise and fall all the time.

The economist Friedrich Hayek famously explained how prices constitute a system of communication that allows markets to allot resources in a way that best meets society's needs and wants. For instance, it's natural for the price of sneakers to rise based on real-world demand for a "hot" new design. Those rising prices signal to producers, stores, and others, that the fancy sneakers are a hit with consumers.

Higher prices also serve another purpose: the lure of potential profits attracts competing sneaker manufacturers to the market. New and even better offerings start popping up. Consumers get more to choose from. Market competition increases, and those hot designs may actually become cheaper. Similarly, if the sneakers fail to sell, discounters will start cutting prices. Manufacturers will stop making those sneakers and redirect their resources into designs that people like better. Rising and falling prices, therefore, are critical to enabling markets to meet the needs of people and create abundance.

Prices tend to rise in an economic expansion where there's increased demand, and decline in a recession when people are tightening their belts and budgets. This is true even when a currency is reliably stable in value. Prices also tend to rise when nations become more prosperous. Prices in Cambodia, for example, are lower than in wealthy Singapore. If Cambodia becomes as wealthy as Singapore, prices in Cambodia would likely rise to Singapore's levels.

Two other examples are Japan and Germany. After World War II, they rebuilt devastated infrastructure, homes, and businesses. The standard of living in both countries improved. Demand for all kinds of goods and services soared. Prices went up.

The increase in prices seen by the US and other nations

in early 2021 was to some extent the result of this "natural" increase in demand. The global economy was starting to recover from an historic trauma caused by a year-long shut-down due to the COVID-19 pandemic. People were beginning to go back to work, travel, eat out, and start shopping again. Labor costs were also rising. Individuals who were thrown out of work were getting new jobs and negotiating higher salaries. Companies were competing with emergency unemployment subsidies that were encouraging employees to stay home.

## Two Kinds of Inflation?

Observers who've attributed pandemic-era price increases to such supply and labor disruptions, therefore, are partly right. That's why it's often said that inflation comes in two varieties: "monetary," and "non-monetary." To understand what's going on in the economy, it's important to know the difference between the two.

**Non-Monetary Inflation.** Some economists call those broad-based price increases resulting from real world changes in supply and demand "non-monetary inflation." This kind of inflation occurs in response to market events. But it usually corrects as markets stabilize. For instance, bad weather leads to impaired crop yields and lower harvests. Prices rise. Farmers looking to cash in increase crop production. What happens? Prices gradually come down.

Non-monetary inflation can also result from artificial shortages created by government interference in a market. Rent controls that discourage new housing construction, for instance, or a government-mandated, higher minimum wage, may both result in higher prices and changes in the CPI. These price increases, too, can come down if regulations are lifted. In other words, non-monetary inflation tends to be a short-term phenomenon that, one way or another, eventually resolves.

However, this kind of inflation is not what we're writing about, and it's not really inflation in the true sense of the word. Inflation, as most people think of it—and as we refer to it here—is not simply price increases. It's about the *distortion* of prices that results from the debasement of money.

Defining inflation simply as "rising prices" does not convey the sense of unease commonly associated with the term—the feeling that *something isn't right* about the prices of goods and services that seem to be shooting up for no apparent reason.

**Monetary Inflation: The Corruption of Money.** Those sneakers that cost $100 a year ago suddenly cost $150. Or your weekly grocery bill used to be $100 and now it's approaching $200. You wonder: Is all of this *really* due to the pandemic? Those grocery bills seem a little too crazy. Besides, things started going up even before COVID. Like that house you bought back in the year 2000 for $600,000. You didn't spend a dime to renovate it and it's in need of repair. No one's flooding into the neighborhood. Plenty of other houses are for sale. Yet in 2021, a little more than two decades later, your house ends up selling for just under $930,000.

You're thrilled about that "profit," until you discover that $930,000 in 2021 will barely get you into another home of comparable value to the one you have just sold. You may even have to put a little cash toward buying something new, or else take a step down.

*That's* inflation. This brings us to a more concise definition:

*Inflation is the distortion of prices that occurs when money loses value.*

*Deflation* is the opposite phenomenon—a drop in prices caused by an *increase* in the value of currency. It occurs far less often, for obvious reasons. Cash-strapped governments are more likely to print and devalue money than to do the opposite.

Monetary inflation and non-monetary inflation each have separate causes and effects. But, as we've seen from the pandemic, both can occur at once. Price increases can be driven simultaneously by monetary and non-monetary factors. The key to understanding what's happening in the economy (and also in your financial life) is knowing how to differentiate between the two. For example, if you've made few, if any, home improvements and the local housing market isn't on fire, you can be sure that the near-million-dollar sale price of your house doesn't mean that it has magically become more valuable. Its worth has been distorted by a gradual, and totally artificial, decline in the value of the dollar.

## Seeing Through Inflation's "Money Illusion"

The price of that hypothetical house may mainly reflect years of low-grade inflation. But people can fail to perceive this reality. They may think that their home's value has appreciated more than it actually has. That's because of what is known as the "Money Illusion," which is the tendency to misinterpret inflation's distorted prices as reflecting "real world" values, instead of what they really are, the consequence of inflation and an ever-shrinking dollar. We assume that the value of money is stable, even when it is not.

It's easy to fall prey to the Money Illusion because we all tend to see our own money as essentially stable. The dollar may be sliding on the currency markets. But in daily life, the greenback is still worth four quarters, or ten dimes, or twenty nickels. Few people appreciate that the dollar's worth on the foreign exchange is also its value in your pocket.

It's far easier to see the effects of inflation on other nations' currencies. For example, if you visited Mexico on vacation back in 1994, a dollar was worth three pesos. If you returned today, you'd get around *twenty* pesos for a dollar. This obvious decline in the value of the peso explains why the cost of souvenirs, not to mention food, gasoline, and other essentials in Mexico has gone up. It also explains why the price increases in terms of pesos are about six-to-seven times more than the increases in terms of dollars. This is the *monetary* inflation that has caused chronic problems throughout Latin America for decades.

Mexico's ever-inflating currency is why the nation's workers find it hard to get ahead. It's also a big reason why no Latin American state (with perhaps the exception of Chile) has reached the status of a developed economy, and why countries like Argentina were relatively wealthier in 1900 than they are today.

**What About the Dollar?** It may be easy to see that the peso is losing value in relation to our own currency. But how do we know what's happening with the dollar? What do we compare *the dollar* to? Economists look at various indicators. They compare the dollar to a basket of consumer goods and services (the CPI), commodity prices, other major currencies like the euro or the British pound, or use other indicators. But, by far, the best one is gold, which served as the United States' premier benchmark of stable monetary value for nearly two centuries.

The yellow metal has long been used to gauge currency value because its intrinsic worth throughout history has remained largely unchanged. Experts estimate that some 7 billion ounces have been mined worldwide and almost all this gold is still accounted for today. Gold's supply relative to demand has held steady; and its worth in relation to the rest of the economy has remained stable. Thus, when the price of gold rises or falls, the changes do not reflect the worth of the yellow metal but *fluctuations in the value of the dollar.*

Former Federal Reserve Chair Alan Greenspan has noted that over the decades, "prices of goods and services fluctuated; but the ratio of gold to the goods and services has remained a relatively constant number."

## Why Gold is a Vital Inflation Indicator

Gold's stable worth in relation to the rest of the economy makes the yellow metal a vital barometer of the worth of the dollar, and the prospects for inflation. When more dollars are needed to buy an ounce of gold, and the trend persists over months or years, that signals the dollar is falling in value. If the CPI, commodity prices, foreign exchange rates, and other indicators are telling the same story, you can be pretty sure that the economy, and many prices, are experiencing a "monetary inflation."

Conversely, gold can also tell you if a deflation reflects a strengthening currency, or simply market pressure on prices.

The gold price is an especially critical indicator because the economy is a complex ecosystem. There can be confusing and sometimes contradictory signals. Gold can cut through the noise. For example, during the Great Recession of 2008-09, the Fed's historic monetary expansion known as Quantitative Easing sent the gold price hurtling past $1,900 an ounce—a serious drop in dollar value and a warning of potential inflation. Yet many consumer prices actually *fell*. Why? Businesses and individuals were still struggling to recover from the financial meltdown of 2008. Fewer were buying and selling. Yet even without a historic crisis, inflation can take time to work its way through the economy.

## Inflation's Telltale Signs

Inflation is often described as "flaring up" and "coming out of nowhere." However, that's not exactly how it happens. A drop in currency value can take time to work its way through the markets.

**Inflation's Slow Creep.** When money loses value, investors and others seeking to preserve their wealth will characteristically buy hard assets—not only gold and other precious metals, but commodities like wheat, lumber, and especially oil. The resulting price increases are first felt by the manufacturers that rely on these products. Some will instantly pass them along to consumers. Retail gasoline prices follow crude oil prices closely. Airline tickets soon reflect changes in the price of jet fuel.

**"Honey, They Shrunk the Dollar."** Producers may try to resist the inflationary pressures of an ever-shrinking dollar by shrinking their products instead. You may notice that you're getting fewer strawberries or potato chips, or there's less cereal in the box. Or maybe that roll of toilet paper is not as wide. Or the sausages you ordered for breakfast at the local diner have gotten smaller. Some have called this phenomenon "shrinkflation."

The discount chain Dollar Tree, which used to sell its products for just a dollar, initially attempted to cope with the post-COVID inflation by using less expensive packaging on some items, and buying certain products in larger quantities to hold down shipping costs. Alas, inflationary pressures can be resisted for only so long. Eventually the chain was forced to raise their prices.

Still, such efforts to hold the line on prices can keep consumers from immediately feeling the effects of inflation. Prices can also take time to move up because of contracts that producers have with employees and suppliers. Wages, for example, are longer-term contracts and tend to increase slowly. As wages rise, corporate costs rise as well. Prices rise more. Rents rise as leases come due. For countries like the US, where businesses often operate based on longer-term contracts, inflation can start off slowly.

Prices accelerate faster in nations with a history of severe inflation. In countries like Mexico or Argentina, for instance, contracts are typically short or written to anticipate rising prices. That gets to another point: the role of human psychology in stoking inflation.

In the summer of 2021, as post-shutdown price increases seemed to be picking up speed, journalist John Steele Gordon issued a warning. "Inflation tends to beget inflation," he wrote. "Once inflationary expectations take hold, they are hard to stop. In the last big inflation, in the 1970s, it took a very steep recession, the worst since the Great Depression, to bring it under control."

## When Money Loses Value

To understand how a currency loses value and causes inflation, it's necessary to appreciate the role of money in the economy. You may have heard numerous definitions of money. We're told that it's a "medium of exchange," "a unit of account," "a store of value," among other things. These definitions, however, miss money's primary function, which is as a *measure* of worth.

Money is a measuring instrument much like a clock, a ruler, or a scale. But instead of measuring time, space, or weight, it measures what something is worth. The Founding Fathers appeared to acknowledge this when they wrote the US Constitution. They described Congress's power to coin and regulate money in the passage that established the standard of weights and measures.

The ancients invented money centuries ago to provide a mutually accepted standard of value that eliminated the messiness of barter. Before the invention of money, a buyer and seller would have to agree, for example, that one's sack of chickens was equal in value to the other's bushel of wheat. Coins eliminated the potential for disputes by providing a mutually agreed-upon unit of worth. Not to mention, they made transactions a lot easier. Instead of buying that sack of wheat with a sack of squawking chickens you could shell out a few coins instead.

The fact that money is, first and foremost, a measuring instrument is illustrated by how people respond when they don't trust their currency. They'll find substitutes. Immediately after World War II, Germans often used cigarettes as money. During the inflation in Italy in the 1970s, candies were traded as small change. Today, citizens of nations suffering extreme inflation will often take dollars or euros in preference to their own government's local currency. Travelers may find that in Vietnam or Peru, the dollar is as widely accepted as the local currency. The reason for this is usually pretty obvious. Look at how many zeros are on the local banknotes.

**What About Cryptos?** Some readers may be wondering: If money is a measuring instrument that must be stable in value, *what about Bitcoin and other cryptocurrencies?* Not everyone will like our answer which is that most cryptos, at least for the present, aren't good money because they're not a reliably stable measure of worth.

Cryptos may have been invented as an alternative to government "fiat" currency. But, at the moment, they're even more turbulent. Bitcoin, for instance, has been known to lose half its value in a single day. If the same slide happened to the dollar or the euro, it would be considered a collapse.

Some businesses may advertise that they accept digital currencies. But how many people do you know who use them regularly to pay for groceries or rent? This is beginning to change. Platforms such as PayPal can instantly convert its merchants' cryptocurrency into dollars. El Salvador, which years ago replaced its currency with the US dollar, has made Bitcoin legal tender. How well the financial infrastructure handles the use of Bitcoin for everyday payments remains to be seen.

Cryptos right now function more like a payment system than an actual currency. However, that may soon change with the rise of a new breed of cryptos known as "stablecoins." They're pegged to a specific asset like the dollar, gold, or commodities. The best-known stablecoin, Tether, is among the biggest cryptos in terms of market value. Right now, currency traders mainly use it, somewhat ironically, to buy the highly volatile Bitcoin. Tether, despite coming under some criticism, is among a handful of digital currencies with true potential to function as real money. But, for now at least, most cryptos are not stable measures of value.

Why is all of this important? Because, for a currency to be in widespread use as "good money," it must be a reliable measure of worth. When it can't fulfill this function, it stops being trusted. And when money is no longer trusted, it eventually loses value. You get inflation.

## CHAPTER TWO

# Not-So-Great Moments in Inflation History

I N CHAPTER ONE we explained that prices can rise for any number of reasons. *Non-monetary* events like supply-chain disruptions, or a spike in demand for a hot product or service—*or* a government regulation that creates scarcity—can all push up prices. The "good" news (if you can call it that) is that the reasons for such price hikes are generally fairly obvious. You'll see media reports, for example, about labor or trucker shortages that may be driving the higher prices. These events tend to be temporary. Sooner or later, those supply chain disruptions will come to an end. Even government constraints that may be pushing up prices—for instance, like rent controls—can be lifted. When the laws are repealed, the shortages will disappear. Prices eventually come down.

However, monetary inflation, *real inflation*—the kind that devastates economies and societies—is something different:

a corruption of prices resulting from the debasement of currency by governments.

**The Second-Oldest Profession.** Currency debasement has been called the world's second-oldest profession because it has been around since the invention of money. The very first coins, minted in Lydia (Turkey) in the seventh century BC, did not contain the gold and silver indicated by their face value.

In ancient times, governments (and also counterfeiters) debased their coins by melting them down and reissuing them with cheaper metal mixed with a lower percentage of gold or silver. This newly created "wealth" might have been worth less than the old currency. But it could fund debt-strapped governments—and the excesses of rulers—at least at first.

**Nero "Fiddles" with Rome's Money.** The Roman emperor Nero (37-68 AD) debased Roman coinage to pay for "riotous" extravagances that included decadent celebrations, lavish palaces, and gifts to friends. In the words of the historian Suetonius, "he made presents and wasted money without stint." Nero debased the Roman denarius by adding copper to the silver coins. This relatively small reduction in value of about 10 percent was just the beginning.

By 260 AD, Rome's increasingly corrupt governments were debasing the coinage to pay their bills. Eventually, the coins contained only 4 percent silver. Then, to keep the game going still further, they minted coins with higher and higher denominations. Naturally, prices rose. According to one account, by the middle of the fourth century, the price of wheat was two million times higher than it had been in the mid-second century. The Roman economy collapsed into hyperinflation.

Soldiers eventually refused to take any more junk coins and only accepted commodities in payment. In the outer reaches of the Roman Empire, the use of money was entirely abandoned. People returned to barter. They also lost the habit of writing. Thus began the Dark Ages.

**China Inflates "the Bark of Trees."** The Chinese, meanwhile, were the first to demonstrate the potential of paper money, which was used briefly around the early ninth century. The first real paper currency, however, was developed two hundred years later by Szechwan merchants. Predictably, China's government soon took over money printing. In the ensuing hyperinflation, the government was overthrown by the nomadic tribes of Manchuria.

The Manchus were also fascinated by the idea of getting bits of paper to pass as money. Unfortunately, when it came to handling this new invention, they did little better than their predecessors. Hyperinflation was followed by the Manchurian government's defeat by the nomadic tribes of Mongolia. After two more governments and two more rounds of hyperinflation, the Chinese finally grew disgusted with paper currencies. Around 1440, China returned to highly reliable copper and silver coinage for the next five hundred years.

The explorer Marco Polo brought China's knowledge of paper money home to Europe. His famed travelogue, *The Travels of Marco Polo,* included a chapter that described "How the Great Khan Causes the Bark of Trees, Made into Something Like Paper, to Pass for Money All Over His Country."

Marco Polo returned to Venice in 1295, but paper money was slow to catch on in Europe. Why debase "the bark of trees" when you can devalue real gold and silver coins?

**Europe: Mercantilism and Inflationism.** Europe's mercantilist monarchs of the sixteenth century were hellbent inflationists who debased their coinages, lowering their values by reducing their silver content. Britain's most infamous coin debaser was King Henry VIII, known for his serial marriages and divorces (including two beheadings). In 1542, he began what was known as the Great Debasement to finance wars with France and Scotland, and also to fund his lavish royal lifestyle. England's once-reliable silver pennies were depleted of about two-thirds of their silver content, sending the price of wheat skyward. Citizens hoarded older coins with higher amounts of precious metal. Foreign vendors demanded payment in bullion, causing a gold shortage and damaging trade. Henry's daughter and eventual successor, Queen Elizabeth I, ultimately turned things around with a new issue of high-quality English silver coinage which remained unchanged for centuries.

**Inflation Sinks the Spanish Empire.** With its territories stretching from California to the Philippines, and its prolific mines in Mexico and Bolivia, Spain led the mercantilist quest for gold and silver in the sixteenth century. Spain's "silver dollars" became the regular coinage of China, the Philippines, and the whole New World from Argentina to the American colonies. All the silver dollars in the world, however, were not enough for Spain's revenue-hungry government. Spain started to debase its domestic coinage beginning in 1599, even as its silver dollars continued to be minted in Mexico City. Thus began a long, sad tale of economic decline. The government struggled to pay its bills by issuing masses of copper coins stamped in ever-higher denominations.

By the 1640s, Spain, which had once stood astride the

world like a Colossus, could barely manage its domestic affairs. At one point, the royal family itself could not raise the funds to travel to its nearby summer residence; sometimes the royal house lacked even bread. The empire disintegrated under the pressure of foreign invasion, domestic secession, and independence movements. Eventually, France replaced Spain as the preeminent power in Europe.

**"Après Moi, le Deluge" of French Hyperinflation.** The famous quote has been attributed to King Louis XV. But it more aptly applies to his great-grandfather, the (misnamed) Sun King, Louis XIV. In the late seventeenth century, the French were on the brink of bankruptcy, thanks to his rampant devaluations and spending. Their eventual solution? Not just more inflation, but one of the most destructive inflationary schemes of all time. Its improbable author was John Law, a Scottish economist, adventurer, and convicted murderer, who had insinuated himself into the upper reaches of French society and later the French government. He persuaded the monarchy that the way to solvency was through exploiting the riches of the New World via the Mississippi Company. This government trading venture would be financed in a new way—through the printing of paper money. What could go wrong?

In a word, *everything*. The company's exploration of what today is Louisiana turned up little more than swampland and mosquitos. When the venture failed to deliver, the "Mississippi Bubble" burst. Shares collapsed, as did the value of France's currency. The catastrophic inflation that ensued forced Law to flee the country. The French stopped using paper money for generations afterwards, returning to using only silver.

**"Not Worth a Continental."** Britain's American colonies were also paper-money abusers and notorious inflaters. In 1690, Massachusetts used paper money to pay soldiers to wage war on the French colony of Quebec. The money was supposedly redeemable later in silver coins. But Massachusetts kept putting off the redeemability date and printing more notes. This strategy was initially so successful that money printing became the rage in the colonies, creating so many monstrous inflations that Britain had to step in and prohibit paper currency.

Not surprisingly, after the American Revolution began in 1775, one of the first acts of the upstart colonists was to bring back paper money to pay soldiers. The first US currency, the Continental dollar, was so over-printed that it became "confetti" and collapsed into hyperinflationary oblivion. For nearly two centuries afterward, "not worth a Continental" was a casual term for worthlessness. Paper money also returned with France's Revolution in 1789. This, too, collapsed in a hyperinflation that led to the ruin of the First Republic. Napoleon Bonaparte stepped in to restore order. In 1800, a new franc was introduced, reliably linked to gold. It remained unchanged until 1914.

The silver lining to these painful debacles was that they led to the rise of Enlightenment thinkers like John Locke and Adam Smith, who awakened people to the folly of inflationism. The American colonists gave up their century-long experiments with government-issued, fiat paper currencies. Later, Alexander Hamilton, the first treasury secretary of the new United States, embraced the principle of a sound and stable dollar.

The moral of these stories: *money is like everything else in an economy. It loses value when there's too much of it.*

## "MONEY PRINTING," HOWEVER, DOES NOT AUTOMATICALLY MEAN INFLATION

The value of a currency, like the value of everything else, is ultimately determined by the ratio between supply and demand. For that reason, the notion that "money printing" inevitably leads to inflation is actually not true. Currency loses value, and inflation ensues, when there is an oversupply of money. But oversupply is different from "large supply."

**The Case of the Swiss Franc.** If a giant money supply was the cause of rising prices, you'd think Switzerland would be overwhelmed by hyperinflation. With a population of just less than nine million, that country has *eight times* more base money per capita than Canada, whose population is nearly four times the size at thirty-eight million.

Instead, the Swiss franc has been one of the world's most reliable currencies over the past hundred years, with less inflation than the US dollar, British pound, euro, or the preceding German mark.

As a result of this track record, many people outside Switzerland are eager to hold assets denominated in Swiss francs. In other words, demand for the Swiss franc is high. To meet this expanding demand, and keep the currency from rising uncomfortably, the Swiss central bank has had to increase supply aggressively.

**A Vibrant Economy, Booming Money Supply—and No Inflation.** When there's sufficient demand, the amount of money in an economy can grow substantially. Between 1775 and 1900, the base money supply of the United States increased by an estimated 163 times. However, the dollar's value (vs. gold) was nearly unchanged. That's right: a 163-times increase in the quantity of money produced no change in the dollar's value.

How was this possible? The answer, once again, is demand. During the 1800s, America experienced exponential growth. Its booming economy had a voracious appetite for money. The nation's first treasury secretary, Alexander Hamilton, had extinguished the wartime hyperinflation that threatened the young nation by establishing a financial system based on stable money; a US dollar pegged to a fixed value of gold. This had turned the once struggling republic into a magnet for investment capital. By the end of the nineteenth century, the US had become the leading industrial power in the world.

Today, the US dollar is a major international currency. Some people think that more than half of all US dollar banknotes in existence are circulating outside the United States. They are in demand by people around the world who consider the dollar to be more reliable than their own domestic currencies.

## No Oversupply, But a Currency "Fail"

Just as a currency can maintain its value despite an exploding money supply, its value can also slide when supply *doesn't* increase. That's what happened in the US in 1933. There was no surge in money printing. Yet the value of the dollar fell 41 percent. Why? Franklin Roosevelt devalued the dollar in an attempt to fight the Great Depression.

Similarly, "money printing" did not precipitate the collapse of the Thai baht and Russian ruble in the late 1990s. The governments of Thailand and Russia had not sought to weaken their currencies. The cause was a drop in demand based on the accurate perception of currency mismanagement—what is known as a "loss of faith" or a "loss of confidence."

However, a government that knows how to manage its currency can prevent faltering confidence from becoming a full-blown disaster. During the Asian crisis of the late 1990s, there were widespread fears that the Hong Kong dollar would succumb to speculative pressures that were dragging down other Asian currencies. That never happened, because Hong Kong's government knew what it was doing. It maintained a stable currency pegged to the US dollar.

## Supply, Demand, and "Loss of Faith"

We explained earlier that money, above all, is a measure of worth that facilitates trade. To fulfill this role, it must be perceived as reliable. It must be *trusted*. An event or a perception that threatens this trust can destroy a currency by triggering what is known as a "loss of faith."

**A Stampede for the Exits.** What can trigger a loss of faith? Anything that suggests that a currency is in danger of losing value. A country faces a calamitous military defeat. Or reckless government spending raises the possibility of a dramatic expansion of the money supply, or an outright currency devaluation. Such circumstances can set off a panic causing people to flee from a currency. They want to be the first out the door before their money declines in value. An extreme loss of faith can result in a disastrous destruction of currency value, precipitating inflation. Two examples include the

South Vietnamese currency, the piastre, which collapsed after the nation's defeat by North Vietnam in the spring of 1975. Similarly, in August 2021, Afghanistan's currency tumbled into near worthlessness when President Joe Biden precipitously withdrew American forces from that country.

Governments and central banks like to imply that a loss of faith is an irrational aberration. In fact, it's anything but. In 1931, when the Bank of England signaled that it would not reduce the money supply to maintain the value of the British pound, the resulting inflationary slide was totally rational. Britain's devaluation raised fears of a devaluation in Japan, which was also in the midst of political turmoil (the country had seized Manchuria from China and had put down a military coup several months earlier). Not surprisingly, a slide in the yen occurred that December.

Loss of faith in a currency can take place without a change in the money supply, or troubles with a government's balance sheet. In the US in the 1960s and 1970s, our federal debt and deficits were minuscule by today's standards. The average budget deficit was 1.3 percent of GDP. The debt-to-GDP ratio was around 35 percent and falling. (Today, it is *127 percent* and rising.) But, during the presidencies of Johnson and then Nixon, it was clear that attempts to manipulate the economy and interest rates were taking precedence over maintaining a stable currency value. People lost trust in the dollar and those that managed it.

This crisis of confidence helped kick off the Great Inflation of the 1970s. Though Richard Nixon had faced a mild inflation at the start of his term, the greenback started to slide in earnest after he severed its link to gold in August 1971. The Nixon Shock meant that the value of the almighty dollar, which had long been the bedrock of the US and global economy, would now float on world currency markets.

Wouldn't you lose confidence, too, if the president himself announced on television that he was essentially throwing the currency to the wolves? This loss of faith was reflected by a jump in the gold price. Between 1970 and 1974, the number of dollars that it took to buy an ounce of gold went from $35 to $175. This surprised economists at the time, because it didn't seem like excessive money printing was a problem. The monetary base—bank reserves and the amount of currency in circulation—grew by only 7 percent in 1971.

The dollar base money supply did increase by 51 percent during the prior decade of the 1960s. But remember, the money supply can expand in response to demand and, in the 1960s, the economy was booming. The value of the dollar remained essentially unchanged.

While the base money supply rose further during the 1970s, the increase was nowhere near enough to account for the collapse in the value of the dollar. Over the course of the decade, the price of gold shot up by more than 2,000 percent. It didn't take long before it also took a lot more dollars to buy commodities like copper, wheat, and oil. The quadrupling of oil prices in 1973-74 was wrongly blamed on Arab retaliation for US support for Israel during the Yom Kippur War. The reality was that Arab oil producers were responding to the plunging dollar by marking up their prices. The Great Inflation—a decade of low growth and rising prices—had begun.

## The "Superstorm" of Hyperinflation

Currency expert Steve Hanke defines hyperinflation as inflation with prices increasing at a rate of 50 percent per month for an extended period of time. Americans generally associate this extreme scenario mainly with 1920s Weimar Germany, or with present-day Venezuela or Argentina. Yet hyperinflation is far more common than most Americans realize. Since the 1980s, these inflationary maelstroms have torn through every country in Latin America, African nations such as Zimbabwe, nearly all the post-Soviet Union republics and even, at one point, the state of Israel. China, Germany, and Japan all experienced bouts of hyperinflation in the aftermath of World War II.

In hyperinflation, an expanding money supply coincides with declining demand, creating an inflation superstorm. Countries "don't know what hit them." No longer able to attract investors who fear a nation's bonds will be rendered worthless, cash-strapped governments will often crank up money printing even further. The notorious hyperinflation in Weimar Germany in the 1920s is the classic illustration of the catastrophic consequences that ensue when "money dies" from an extreme loss of faith.

After Germany's defeat in World War I, the European allies demanded the nation pay war reparations in the Treaty of Versailles of 1919. To generate funds for this gargantuan debt, and also to pay government workers, Germany powered up the printing press. Between January 1919 and February 1920, the monetary base increased by 58 percent. People could see where this was going. The currency's value imploded. Over those thirteen months, the number of German marks that it took to buy one US dollar (which at the time was linked to gold) increased by eleven times. This was only the beginning.

One way to see how much the demand for German marks

fell is to measure the value of the entire German money supply in terms of gold-backed US dollars. In January 1919, the German money supply was worth $6.25 billion. In January 1922, it was worth only $1.12 billion. As the hyperinflation of late 1922-1923 intensified, the value of the German money supply collapsed to $101 million. Further exacerbating the disaster was even more money printing by the German central bank, whose bureaucrats labored under the irrational belief that the problem was a currency *shortage*, and that still more money printing was needed to keep up with the rise in prices.

The dramatic slide in the value of the German mark produced higher prices that undermined confidence in the currency and sent Germans into a panic that fed on itself. People rushed to preserve their wealth by buying any hard assets they could get their hands on. Adam Fergusson famously recounted in *When Money Dies*, his classic history of the Weimar hyperinflation, that people bought pianos who couldn't play them. The feverish activity sent prices even higher. At its height, the mark's hyperinflation rate reached an astonishing level of nearly 30,000 percent *per month*. Prices were doubling every three or four days. In Fergusson's words: "You'd go to a restaurant and you find that your meal is going to cost eight thousand marks and you order it, you eat it, and by the time the bill comes, that eight thousand marks has become sixteen thousand."

In November 1923, the old currency was thrown out and replaced with a new currency that was linked to gold. That is typical of many nations beset by hyperinflation. Some countries that have suffered hyperinflation, such as El Salvador and Ecuador, have abandoned their currencies in favor of the US dollar.

## Why Hyperinflation Is Not Just "More Inflation"

Most people think of hyperinflation as *inflation gone wild*. That's basically true. But there are important distinctions. In a serious inflation, such as the monetary malaise experienced during the 1970s, the money supply growth is not of the magnitude of a hyperinflation. The Nixon Shock, for example, was intended as a short-term, Keynesian stimulus to lift the economy out of a mild recession.

In hyperinflation, however, money printing is not temporary, but employed as the principal method of government finance. This is illustrated by the Weimar hyperinflation. Germany's money printing went beyond just paying reparations to its former World War I adversaries. In 1922, 63 percent of the nation's total government spending was financed by the printing press. Shutting down the printing press would have meant shutting down 63 percent of the government overnight.

The same addiction to money printing bedevils present-day hyperinflaters like Venezuela and Argentina. In these countries, printing money is part of the routine operation of government, like taxes. This continual decline in a currency results in a cost-of-living which spirals upwards without end, distorting not only the economy but every aspect of life.

## "Inflationism" in the Modern Era

Fortunately, this kind of nightmare has been outside the experience of Americans—so far. Throughout the nineteenth and into the early twentieth centuries, a long list of countries, including Britain, the United States, Italy, Austria, Russia, Brazil, Argentina, Chile, Spain, Portugal, Greece, and Japan had brief periods of floating currencies, usually because of war. But most of them eventually returned to "sound money" linked to gold. Sound money, "as good as gold," was considered the ideal.

However, with the Great Depression in the 1930s, this thinking began to change. Despite the inflationary disasters that roiled Germany and other countries after World War I, "inflationism" returned. This time it was not only respectable; it was perceived as a *moral good*.

**The Rise of Keynes.** When Franklin Roosevelt took office in 1933, he devalued the dollar in an effort to resuscitate the struggling economy. His objective, as reported by the *New York Times*, was "to lift prices and aid our trade position." FDR confiscated the gold of US citizens and then began to devalue the dollar by 41 percent, from $20.67 to $35 per ounce of gold. This did not work very well, as the Great Depression dragged on through the 1930s. Yet that did little to change the perception that the Depression was a failure of "unstable" markets, and that the solution lay with government activism.

The British economist John Maynard Keynes rose to prominence by advancing the idea that the government could create economic prosperity through a mix of government spending and changing the value of the currency. Despite his influence, however, he lost the debate over a return to the gold standard.

In 1944, dismayed by the devaluations and floating currencies that erupted into turmoil in the 1930s, the world's nations got together at the Mount Washington Hotel, in

Bretton Woods, NH, to establish a new, postwar, global gold standard system.

Keynes died two years later, in 1946, but his ideas continued to be refined by his followers. The idea of inflation as a positive force continued to gain traction. In the 1950s, New Zealand economist William Phillips came up with the Phillips Curve, which linked periods of prosperity and "full employment" to heightened levels of inflation. This backwards thinking led President Richard Nixon, and his Fed Chair Arthur Burns, to adopt an "easy money" strategy in response to the mild 1970 recession. In January 1971, Nixon declared that he was "now a Keynesian in economics." A few months later, America's commitment to sound money and the Bretton Woods gold standard came to an end.

Keynesianism fell out of favor after the Great Inflation of the 1970s. The Phillips Curve was disproved by a succession of Nobel-prize winning economists. Unfortunately, bad ideas can be the hardest to kill. In the first decades of the twenty-first century, calling oneself a "Keynesian" is considered somewhat old-fashioned, but Keynesian policies live on. The US and other nations rely on unstable "fiat" currencies—and inflationism has returned with a vengeance.

## THE FAILURES OF THE KEYNESIAN FED

The US Federal Reserve central banking system was founded in 1913 after the Panic of 1907. The original mandate of this new entity was to serve as "a lender of last resort" for the nation's lending institutions that could prevent the kind of bank runs that had caused that crisis. The Fed was to provide liquidity to banks to meet the seasonal cash needs of America's large agricultural economy. Finally, the central bank was also to protect the stability of the dollar and ward off inflation.

Today that mission sounds quaint. Over the course of more than a century, the Fed has dramatically increased its activism. The Employment Act of 1946 required the federal government to deal with inflation and unemployment. This was interpreted to apply to Federal Reserve policy. In the late 1970s, Congress required the Federal Reserve to adopt a Keynesian "dual mandate" to achieve "stable prices and full employment" through manipulating interest rates and the supply of money. No longer was the Fed's goal to maintain a stable dollar. It was to guide the economy. Think we're headed for a downturn? Pump in cheap money. Things looking a little frothy? Tighten up.

Consisting of twelve regional Federal Reserve Banks, the Fed is where the nation's banks park their cash, or so-called "reserves." When the central bank wants to pump money into the economy, it engages in a process known as "open market operations" (OMOs). That involves buying securities, mainly government bonds ("Treasuries") from the financial institutions like investment banks that are the "primary dealers" of those securities. To buy the bonds, the Fed will often digitally create money "out of thin air." The process is essentially a twofer: it expands the money supply by channeling money to the banks that they can lend. Meanwhile Uncle Sam—the bond issuer—gets money to pay his bills.

When the Fed wants to "tighten up," or reduce the money supply, it reverses this procedure, *selling* bonds to the banks. The banks buy the bonds. Their money goes back to the Fed—and disappears.

Central banks today are ostensibly independent. They're supposed to operate free from political pressure by politicians wanting more money for larger government. Yet that's not what's happening. Noted economist Judy Shelton observes in the *Wall Street Journal*, that "with the Fed owning roughly one-quarter of the federal debt held by the public on which the Treasury must pay interest—and with the Fed's practice of sending weekly remittances to Treasury—it's clear that monetary and fiscal policy are conflated."

In other words, Washington relies on a constant flow of zero-interest-rate "free loans" from Federal Reserve bond buying/money creation. (In addition, virtually all the interest payments on the bonds—now over $90 billion a year—goes back to the Treasury.) This Fed-enabled borrowing encourages a vicious inflationary cycle (see illustration), leading to larger government, more spending, and debt. This in turn increases pressure on the Fed to create still more money to keep those interest-free loans coming.

This is why some fear that, in the foreseeable future, the Federal Reserve will be tempted to keep interest rates artificially low, with only minor increases. Unfortunately, this appears to be where things are headed, and not just in the US. Governments elsewhere are seeking cheap loans and increasingly expecting central banks to hold down interest rates. And so-called "independent" central banks are complying. They are buying bonds to effectively fund governments—creating too much money and encouraging inflation.

## From "Keynesianism" to "Inflation on Steroids"

For decades, the Fed had used open market operations to guide the economy largely through regulating interest rates. The presumption was that lowering interest rates would

## Figure 1

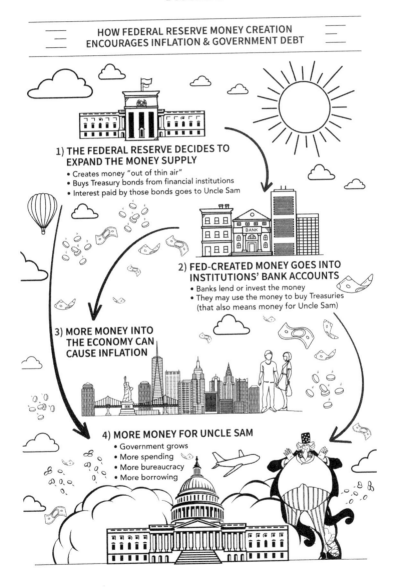

HOW FEDERAL RESERVE MONEY CREATION
ENCOURAGES INFLATION & GOVERNMENT DEBT

**1) THE FEDERAL RESERVE DECIDES TO EXPAND THE MONEY SUPPLY**
- Creates money "out of thin air"
- Buys Treasury bonds from financial institutions
- Interest paid by those bonds goes to Uncle Sam

**2) FED-CREATED MONEY GOES INTO INSTITUTIONS' BANK ACCOUNTS**
- Banks lend or invest the money
- They may use the money to buy Treasuries (that also means money for Uncle Sam)

**3) MORE MONEY INTO THE ECONOMY CAN CAUSE INFLATION**

**4) MORE MONEY FOR UNCLE SAM**
- Government grows
- More spending
- More bureaucracy
- More borrowing

stimulate economic activity by reducing the cost of borrowing. Raising rates would dampen it. But in the twenty-first century, the use of this Keynesian "tool" reached a magnitude never before envisioned. The turning point was the financial crisis and Great Recession that began in 2008.

Previously, open market operations were employed mainly to regulate the money supply by either lowering ("easing") or raising *short-term* interest rates. But following the financial crisis of 2008, the Fed engaged in a new version of this strategy known as "Quantitative Easing" (QE). Instead of targeting short-term rates, the Fed bought *long-term* Treasuries and mortgage-backed securities in unprecedented quantities. These gargantuan purchases enabled the Fed, and other central banks that engaged in QE, to get historically low interest rates, which collapsed to near zero. The intention was to shore up a shaky financial system and bring about a recovery by dramatically lowering the cost of borrowing.

In effect, the Fed was ramping up the easy-money strategy which helped create the housing bubble that started the financial crisis in the first place. Few observers at the time, however, noted this irony. In a speech in 2012, then Fed Chair Ben Bernanke explained how that unusual move had been inspired by an observation by the Keynesian economist James Tobin. Years earlier, he had suggested that "purchases of longer-term securities by the Federal Reserve during the Great Depression could have helped the US economy recover."

The Fed's QE strategy had profound implications. Instead of regulating rates and money by moving in and out of short-term securities, the Federal Reserve and other central banks were now powerful, long-term creditors with a more influential role in the economy. Some central banks, notably in

Japan and Switzerland, even started to buy corporate equities or Real Estate Investment Trusts. The US and other once-prudent governments, emboldened by central banks that seemed to be effectively financing their deficits by buying their debt, ran the largest peacetime deficits ever.

Also propelling the Fed's move were new global banking regulations under the "Basel III" international regulatory accord. First adopted in 2010, the new rules were intended to prevent another 2008-style crisis by requiring banks to substantially increase their cash reserves. Central banks therefore had to expand their money supply dramatically to accommodate banks' enhanced need for dollars. To further encourage banks to expand their protective cushion of reserves, the Fed, in another unprecedented move, started paying interest on these balances.

James Grant, editor of *Grant's Interest Rate Observer*, explains that as a consequence, "A great deal of these trillions were locked up in inert accounts at the Federal Reserve. [ ... ] Dollars that might as well be in deep freeze [ ... ] they didn't circulate."

**The "Inflation" That Wasn't.** This "deep freeze" was the reason why QE, despite widespread fears, failed to bring on a 1970s-level inflation or hyperinflation. Nonetheless, a new perception was emerging: that the Fed could print prodigious amounts of money without the economy suffering inflationary consequences.

## And the Band Plays On ...

Between 2008 and early 2021, the US monetary base—currency in circulation and bank reserves— exploded from $830 billion to over $6 trillion. The Federal Reserve created more than $5 trillion out of thin air. Most of this was the one-time windfall related to those new banking regulations. Some was due to the natural needs of a growing economy, including a large increase in dollar banknotes being used outside the United States. Nonetheless, by mid-2021, banks had more cash than the new regulations required.

Yet, the Fed and other central banks still didn't show much eagerness to take their foot off the pedal and ease up on the money creation. They feared a big increase in interest rates could cause another downturn. And while the recession may have been over, the spending wasn't. Not only the US, but other nations too, have continued to run huge deficits.

The historic monetary expansion produced, in a little more than ten years, a substantial drop in the value of the dollar. Between 2008 and 2020, the value of the dollar fell in half, as the price of gold shot up from around $900 per ounce to around $1,800 per ounce. Yet, central banks publicly worried that there wasn't enough inflation!

**"Sterilizing" Money Creation via "Reverse Repos."** In 2021, the Fed was still buying $120 billion in Treasuries and mortgage-backed securities *per month*. Yet, interestingly, this was taking place without further driving up the gold price and weakening the dollar. How was the central bank able to do this? Through something called a "reverse repurchase agreement," or, "reverse repo." In this little-known maneuver, the Fed buys Treasury bonds and mortgage-backed securities, sending money into the banks. Then, it turns around and *borrows* back the money, using Treasuries as collateral. This ends up removing the money from the system. But remember, the banks are officially loaning the money to the Fed. Within a short period, often overnight, the central bank pays them back, with interest.

In this way, money sloshes back and forth. The process enables the Fed to buy billions in bonds without increasing the money supply. A reverse repo is the equivalent of pouring a bucket of water into a pool at one end and removing the water at the other end. The end effect is to neutralize the impact of the Fed's bond buying, preventing an increase in the money supply that could trigger a drop in the value of the dollar.

In February of 2021, the Fed had very few reverse repos on its balance sheet. By December, the number had swelled to more than $1.7 trillion. Reverse repos have so far received little notice. Yet they are enabling the Federal Reserve to continue expanding its balance sheet by buying government bonds. The exercise holds down interest rates and facilitates reckless government borrowing. What if there's an event, like a sudden military crisis, and Uncle Sam can't meet its obligations? You would see a financial crisis that would make 2008 look like a hiccup.

## "Why Can't We Just Print More Money?"

If the US can expand the supply of money without creating inflation, why can't we just print more money to fund government programs to ostensibly help the poor and save the planet? That question is at the heart of Modern Monetary Theory (MMT), currently the rage among socialist "Progressives" like Congresswoman Alexandria Ocasio-Cortez, Senator Bernie Sanders, and many within the Biden administration, including the president himself. When Joe Biden insisted that the US could prevent inflation through more government spending, he was parroting this misguided idea.

MMT has been around for a while. But it has garnered renewed attention because of its high-profile supporters and publication of *The Deficit Myth: Modern Monetary Theory and the Birth of the People's Economy* by Stony Brook University economist Stephanie Kelton.

Kelton believes the government can easily afford a "People's Economy," a welfare state with a cornucopia of freebies and programs like the Green New Deal. Uncle Sam can just keep spending because in her words, "he can't run out of money." Federal Reserve bond buying and money creation, she insists, can go on almost indefinitely. After all, isn't that what we're already doing?

Kelton cites the example of Japan. Its central bank holds 50 percent of that nation's government bonds—twice the percentage of US federal debt held by the Fed—with interest rates near zero. Yet, like the US, Japan, she says, is doing just fine.

But what about Japan's humongous debt? Simple, she says. All the Bank of Japan has to do is create bank reserves to buy all of Japan's bonds, thereby cancelling the government's obligations. With just "a one-time flick of the wand," or a keyboard stroke, she writes, "Poof! The debt is gone."

Kelton doesn't deny that inflation is a concern. But she insists that it can be controlled by creating "an economy that is productive enough to supply the mix of goods and services we'll need." How does she intend to do this? Through more government programs and taxes.

**Old Wine in New Bottles.** What do we say to this? There's nothing "modern" about Modern Monetary Theory. If anything, it sounds more like Venezuela today or France in the eighteenth century. If the Fed printed money nonstop to fund Kelton's welfare-state vision, investors and anyone else holding dollars would run for the hills. The dollar would go the way of the Russian ruble in the '90s or the Cuban peso.

When have higher taxes and a larger government bureaucracy produced a healthy economy and low inflation? Kelton is essentially describing what goes on in countries like Venezuela, or for that matter Argentina or Cuba, where bloated governments are routinely financed by money printing. Once you have, in principle, unshackled the government from any need to limit its spending, and start arguing that you can have all the benefits of spending money without the unpleasantness of taxing and borrowing, the sky's the limit. Kelton's vision of a "people's economy" funded by the magical conjuring of money is a surefire formula for *hyperinflation*.

*The famed "WIN" button, a symbol of President Gerald Ford's
1974 campaign to "Whip Inflation Now."*

## CHAPTER THREE

# Why Inflation Is Bad

W HY DO WE SAY that inflation is *bad*? Many in the economic establishment would disagree. They insist that inflation, at low levels, is actually *good*.

In the summer of 2020, with millions out of work as a result of pandemic-related shutdowns, Federal Reserve Chair Jerome Powell announced that the Fed would allow prices to rise beyond the normal rate of 2 percent that the central bank believes constitutes "stability." Acknowledging that, "Many find it counterintuitive that the Fed would want to push up inflation," Powell went on to explain that "low and stable inflation is essential for a well-functioning economy."

He added, "[W]e are certainly mindful that higher prices for essential items, such as food, gasoline, and shelter, add to the burdens faced by many families, especially those struggling with lost jobs and incomes. However, inflation that is persistently *too low* can pose serious risks." (Our italics.)

Powell's counterintuitive beliefs are echoed throughout

the economic establishment. One economics professor interviewed by the website Marketplace.org asserted that, in the website's words, "lack of inflation can create problems for consumers, because when prices fall, wages are likely to fall as well, since firms are earning less for what they sell." That certainly didn't seem to be the case before the pandemic, when inflation was less than 2 percent, and income growth soared. In 2019, median household income grew by 6.8 percent, the largest increase on record.

Yet economists, and many in the media, keep touting the supposed benefits of inflation. A few years back, during the Great Recession, the *New York Times* applauded a return to Keynesian inflationism. Their story declared: "In Fed and Out, Many Now Think Inflation Helps."

> The school board in Anchorage, Alaska, for example, is counting on inflation to keep a lid on teachers' wages. Retailers including Costco and Walmart are hoping for higher inflation to increase profits. The federal government expects inflation to ease the burden of its debts.

The paper quoted Harvard economist Ken Rogoff who opined, "a sustained burst of moderate inflation is not something to worry about." In fact, he added, "It should be embraced."

Really? We wonder if anyone cared to ask Richard Dixson his thoughts about this conventional wisdom. Dixson and his wife live in Kansas City, MO. The couple, who care for four young grandchildren, have seen diaper bills skyrocket to $300 a month. The higher prices have become such a burden that the middle-aged couple has had to cut back on necessities.

Or, how about Melissa Roberts, a young mother of four struggling to get by in a Chicago suburb. Her partner lost his job as a furniture salesman in the pandemic. Soaring food prices have caused household fights over high grocery bills and forced the family to adopt a cheaper, less healthy diet with less real meat and fewer fresh fruits and vegetables.

What about the poor in nations like Cambodia, where upwardly spiraling food prices have caused widespread hunger and starvation, exacerbating the nightmare of COVID.

If you asked these people, we doubt they would see any benefit in rising prices. They'd be right. The Fed's policy of pumping up prices is "counterintuitive," to use Jerome Powell's word, because it's the opposite of common sense. There's nothing good about 2 percent, 5 percent, or any rate of inflation.

## BACKWARD THINKING AT THE FED

Why are Fed officials in love with the idea that creating "a little inflation" will make people richer? The influential and highly persuasive British economist John Maynard Keynes first advanced the notion that manipulating money would bring about full employment, just in time for the Great Depression. The idea, while misguided, was in line with the *zeitgeist* of a nation yearning to end rampant joblessness— not to mention the ambitions of central bankers for greater influence over the economy. Sadly, for us, the notion has stuck around ever since.

**Behind the (Phillips) Curve.** Keynes's ideas about inflation and employment began to gain real traction in the 1950s. New Zealand economist William Phillips unveiled a graph that became known as the Phillips Curve. It showed an apparent correlation between higher inflation and lower unemployment. His conclusion was that inflation equaled job creation.

The problem with the Phillips Curve is that it is based on thinking that, you might say, is behind the curve. Seven Nobel prizes have been awarded to economists whose work *disproved* the theory. Economic historian Brian Domitrovic has pointed out on Forbes.com that the numbers show that inflation does not create employment and is associated with the reverse—higher jobless rates.

During the inflationary early 1980s, Domitrovic notes, unemployment peaked at a higher level than during the financial crisis of 2008. After money has been cheapened, there may be an initial flurry of activity and some job creation. But this quickly subsides.

Contrary to Keynesian belief, low unemployment coincides with periods of stable money and minimal inflation. The United States experienced what could be characterized as full employment (jobless rates of less than 5 percent) during the gold standard years of the 1920s and 1960s.

Job creation boomed, along with the economy, in the 1980s after Ronald Reagan ended inflation by stabilizing the dollar and cutting taxes. Another example is Switzerland, whose currency has been the best at maintaining its value over the past one hundred years with no evidence of the Phillips Curve. The country's unemployment rate hovers around 3 percent.

**Cargo Cult Thinking.** Yes, it's true that economic growth can mean higher prices for certain products. But the notion that pushing up the cost of living will produce prosperity is *cargo cult thinking* that confuses correlation and causation.

Equally nonsensical is the idea that low inflation somehow endangers the economy. Has anyone ever complained about laptops or flat-screen TVs getting cheaper?

**A "Golden" Age with No Inflation.** If no inflation is "bad," then how does one account for the explosion of prosperity that took place during the nineteenth-century era of the classical gold standard, a period in our history that is largely forgotten today? With isolated exceptions, including America's suspension of the gold standard during the Civil War, the US during the late nineteenth century experienced periods where prices actually declined. Yet the nation nevertheless enjoyed a 100-year boom.

The stable, gold-based dollar established by Alexander Hamilton meant that investors could count on getting repaid in money that had not lost value. That encouraged lending and investment. The US became a magnet for foreign capital. Dollars flowed into new, growth-creating ventures, boosting productivity and innovation, leading to lower prices. Between 1870 and 1890, the cost of steel production fell by a factor of six. World steel production soared twenty times higher. Cheap steel poured into new railways and skyscrapers in growing cities. During the 1880s, the United States added more than 7,000 miles of new railway per year. The cost of transportation plummeted.

More steel also went into the new automobiles, like the Ford Model T, introduced in 1908 for a mere $850. By 1925, as Henry Ford perfected his new assembly-line methods, the car's price had fallen to $260. In the 1850s, whale oil (commonly used for lighting) cost about $1.75 a gallon. In 1870, kerosene replaced whale oil at $0.26 per gallon. By 1911, a gallon of kerosene cost 9.2 cents. This kind of *deflation* made the United States the wealthiest country in the world by 1913.

Following the example of the United States and England, most of Europe and eventually Japan pegged their currencies to gold. More wealth was created in the 1800s than all the previous centuries put together.

**Why You Can't Devalue Your Way to Prosperity.** Keynes argued that inflation would increase employment by reducing the real value of wages, making it cheaper to hire workers. This may happen initially. Yet while devaluing currency appears to "raise" salaries, it also pushes up living expenses. Workers can afford less, and eventually the economy suffers.

In the words of Steve Hanke, the currency expert from Johns Hopkins University, "If devaluations caused so much growth, you would think that Africa would be booming [and] South America would be leading the world." Former congressman Ron Paul once put it this way: "If governments or central banks really can create wealth simply by creating money, why does poverty exist anywhere on earth?"

## INFLATION'S MONSTROUS UNFAIRNESS

Keynesian wisdom about the supposed need for low inflation gets everything backwards. How does lowering the value of the dollar in your pocket make you or anybody else richer?

**A "Stealth Tax."** Of course, it can't. That's why many economists have called inflation a "stealth tax." Keynes himself famously acknowledged that devaluing money enables government to "confiscate, secretly and unobserved, an important part of the wealth of their citizens."

Take a hypothetical nurse with an income of $50,000. A rate of 2 percent annual inflation—a level the Fed defines as "stability"—means a rise in the cost of living that will result in $1,000 being effectively deducted from that nurse's annual salary. Think of this as a new form of withholding.

**"Inflation Inequality."** Inflation's stealth tax punishes people on fixed salaries, savers, retirees on pensions—the people who play by the rules. It does this not only by eroding their incomes, but also by driving up prices of the goods and services that they especially rely on. Stony Brook University professor and social scientist Todd Pittinsky has noted that "prices often increase more for basic needs than for luxury items, a phenomenon economists call 'inflation inequality.'" His observation is confirmed by studies showing that inflation increases income inequality as measured by indicators like the Gini coefficient.

At the same time that it hurts those on lower incomes, inflation delivers windfalls to sophisticated individuals and corporations, especially financial companies, that can navigate an environment of changing currency value. While the poor get poorer, the rich get richer. Noted economist and author Mark Skousen, citing Ludwig von Mises, points out that those who most benefit are generally the first recipients of Fed-created money. Who falls into this category? Skousen replies that the beneficiaries include "big banks, commercial interests, stock market investors, Wall Street."

Inflation also creates a revenue bonanza for government. As rising wages push people into higher tax brackets, Uncle Sam collects more in taxes. 2021 saw the biggest one-year increase in federal tax receipts since the late 1970s. People on Main Street may be struggling to adjust to higher prices. But government bureaucrats benefit from inflation's gusher of money.

**Another Point About Those "Higher Wages"** The COVID crisis provides a powerful illustration of inflation's fundamental unfairness. In October of 2021, the *Wall Street Journal* reported certain sectors, like real estate, appeared to be booming. Yet at the same time, "workers are paying the price." While their paychecks seemed to be rising, "real hourly earnings"—the buying power of their dollars—*fell* by nearly 2 percent within the space of one year. According to eye-opening calculations from the University of Pennsylvania, the average US household spent *$3,500 more* keeping up with inflation.

Little wonder that the philosopher John Locke famously called currency devaluation a "public failure of justice" that gives "one man's right and possession to another."

## An Enabler of Debt

Inflation unfairly tips the scales against lenders in favor of debtors. People with fixed obligations like rents or mortgages get to pay back loans with cheaper money. Compared with the rest of the economy's inflated values, what you owe suddenly appears more reasonable. Thus, inflation is often called an "enabler of debt."

That's why, in countries that are big inflaters, you usually see astronomical interest rates. No one wants to lend money when you will be paid back in a currency of lesser value. In 2021, Argentina had an annual inflation rate of more than 51 percent and an interest rate of 38 percent. Turkey, which had a more moderate inflation rate (relatively) of more than 20 percent, had an interest rate of 15 percent. In the US during the inflationary 1970s, when the value of the dollar was plummeting, interest rates reached nearly 22 percent.

**Finance Destroyed.** In countries like Venezuela and Argentina that have a history of devaluation and hyperinflation, financing is virtually nonexistent, except for companies large enough to attract foreign capital or have the political connections to get government subsidies or loans. Credit cards, consumer debt, home mortgages, and small business loans are unavailable, or available only at usurious interest rates. Cooperation between lenders and borrowers becomes nearly impossible. Even governments can't borrow except at nosebleed interest rates and short maturities of less than a year.

**The Further Distortion of "Zero Interest Rates."** In the twenty-first century, the distortion of inflation has been exacerbated by an alarming first—artificially low interest rates brought about by central banks. Didn't we just say that inflation is traditionally accompanied by *higher* interest rates? Yes, we did, and that is still the case in nations with the worst inflation. Yet, since 2008, the Fed and other central banks have been defying this norm. Ignoring inflation, they have pushed interest rates down to some of the lowest levels ever seen in recorded history.

Intended to stimulate the economy by encouraging loans at bargain basement rates, the strategy is essentially Keynes on steroids. The result has been a distortion of capital markets. Small borrowers are penalized. Why should banks unable to get a return from zero-interest-rate lending take a chance on risky newcomers? They'll favor well-heeled individuals or large corporations that are sure credit risks, including those that don't really need to borrow. The big players end up getting loans that are essentially free.

The computer giant Apple has taken on tens of billions of dollars in debt, even though it has net cash of some $80 billion. Over a period of eight years, the company used virtually free money to buy back some $444 billion of its own stock, reducing the share count by 35 percent, which has helped boost its price and dividends.

Of course, the biggest debtor is the US government, whose total federal debt in early 2021 was around $29 trillion. Inflation, combined with zero-interest-rate free money means that Uncle Sam saves billions on its payments to bond holders. These savings enable the government to spend more on its already-bloated bureaucracies and runaway entitlement programs.

More programs mean more spending and eventually more borrowing and, thus, more money creation. It's a vicious inflationary cycle. As Johns Hopkins political scientist Josef Joffe has observed, "Inflation is the best way to make the public debt melt away and keep the floodgates open. The downside? Devalued dollars make the masses poorer and more dependent on the government."

## Markets Misled by the Money Illusion

Earlier we explained how inflation corrupts the price signals that are critical to market perceptions of supply and demand. People misled by inflation's Money Illusion will often misinterpret inflationary prices as indicating real-world values.

They make decisions to buy or invest based on what is essentially misinformation. Inflation's distortion of money ends up distorting market behavior.

**The "Energy Shortage" That Wasn't.** The fuel crisis of the 1970s is a textbook example of the destructive effects of the Money Illusion. The devaluation of the US dollar after the Nixon Shock quickly pushed up prices on the commodities markets that are traditionally first to feel the devaluation of currency.

From 1973 to 1975, oil rose from its longtime level of about $3 per barrel to more than $12 per barrel. This triggered concerns that the world was running out of energy. Fear verged on near panic. *Newsweek* declared in a cover story that the US was "Running Out of Everything."

The "energy crisis" and its endless lines at the gas pump were widely blamed on the Arab Oil Embargo. That was the Money Illusion. Economist Brian Domitrovic explains that the supposed scarcity "was a currency crisis, not an oil crisis." In other words, it was a direct result of the devaluation of the dollar.

He points to a letter from the secretary general of OPEC, the Middle East oil cartel, that was written days after the US abandoned the gold standard, warning that "member countries of OPEC will take the necessary steps *to adjust crude oil posted prices accordingly*" if the floating dollar dropped in value on the foreign exchange markets. (Our italics.)

Had the US returned to a sound-and-stable dollar after the Nixon Shock, Domitrovic says, the country would have never seen a fuel crisis. The price of a gallon of gas "would not have exceeded fifty cents."

## Inflation's Funhouse Mirrors

The housing bubble that led to the implosion of the subprime mortgage market and the 2008 financial crisis was another result of the Money Illusion created by inflation. The story began in the early 2000s with the recession that followed the collapse of tech stocks known as the "dotcom bust." In an attempt to stimulate the economy, the Fed, in a series of steps, lowered the federal funds rate to 1 percent. Between 2000 and 2003 the monetary base grew at levels equivalent to the inflationary 1970s. The dollar slid in value. The price of gold moved sharply upward.

Remember, when money is devalued, the first place it goes is into hard assets like housing. Homeowners were big winners in the 1970s inflation, which pushed up house prices while mortgage payments were inflated away. The lure of housing as an investment may have been even greater in the early 2000s, when the Fed's cheap money encouraged banks to practically give away mortgages. They loosened lending standards, making more loans to higher-risk, subprime borrowers. The subprime mortgage market grew by 200 percent.

Inflation's herd instinct took hold among buyers and sellers. No longer were home buyers asked for the traditional 20 percent down before buying a house. "Stated income loans" became common. They were also known as "no-doc" or "liar loans" because borrowers could give just about any income figure and it was rarely checked. Little wonder just about everyone wanted to get in on the action. A homeless man in St. Petersburg, FL, managed to buy five houses. Speculators rushed into the market. The weak dollar corrupted pricing information, leading people to believe that housing prices and demand could only go up. As prices rose, there seemed little risk of default. Even if homeowners fell behind on their mortgages, they could sell their houses for more than they had bought them for, and repay the loan. *So what* if a homeless investor defaulted? The house would be worth more than his mortgage.

In 2005, the Fed started to raise interest rates. The market fell apart. Foreclosures rolled through every state in the union. As many as 10 million people were said to have lost their homes. The devastation shook major financial institutions. The investment houses Lehman Brothers and Bear Stearns collapsed, followed by the forced sale of Merrill Lynch. AIG, the largest commercial insurer, and Citibank were taken over by the US government. The S&P 500 stock index saw a 58 percent drop. The 2008 financial crisis was followed by the "Great Recession," the biggest economic downturn since the Great Depression.

## GOOD BUBBLES AND BAD BUBBLES

Every industry experiences shake-outs when, for whatever reason, too many players enter a market. That can happen when there's a new and promising technology, like the PC boom in the early 1980s, auto manufacturing in the early twentieth century or, for those who remember the 1950s, the hula hoop craze. In a normal economy, businesses fail. However, people learn from such setbacks. The players that survive are more efficient and usually do things better. That's how knowledge is acquired and industry—and society—advances.

But inflationary bubbles are something else: fake activity arising from a misdirection of capital. Individuals and businesses make decisions based on distorted price signals, like those home buyers during the early 2000s who were convinced that housing prices could only go up. Inflationary price signals can also create a rush into nonproductive investments whose primary purpose is wealth preservation. Money tends to flow into hard assets such as gold bullion. Citizens desperate to preserve their rapidly dwindling wealth will plow it into whatever commodities or other tangibles that happen to be on hand.

The classic example: Germans who bought pianos during the Weimar inflation. Impoverished citizens of the old Soviet Union and Eastern Europe would stockpile bricks. They weren't perishable and could be used at some point in the future. With money being inflated away, saving currency was untenable. Johns Hopkins economist Steve Hanke explains that instead of saving money at the bank, "you had a brick account."

## TAXES ARE INFLATED, TOO

The Money Illusion similarly corrupts taxation. In the 1970s, middle-income people suddenly found that they had been pushed into higher tax brackets. The tax system was designed for a stable currency. There were no automatic "inflationary adjustments," which were introduced in the 1980s. People hadn't really gotten raises. Their "higher" pay was in inflated dollars.

Uncle Sam didn't care. Ordinary citizens were socked with taxes meant for the rich. A family of four making twice the median income had a marginal tax rate of 25 percent in 1965. That rate rose to 43 percent in 1980. The phenomenon was known as "bracket creep."

Corporations and investors were similarly taxed on "capital gains" that weren't gains at all, but inflationary illusions. During the 1970s, the *real* tax on capital gains, when taking inflation into account, could exceed 100 percent. People and companies got hit by capital gains taxes when the real value of their assets had actually *declined.*

According to one estimate, if you had bought an S&P 500 index fund in 1970 and sold it in 1988, the effective *real* capital gains tax rate on your investment would be *338 percent* due to inflation during that period.

Inflation also hurt existing ventures in the 1970s by eroding the tax benefit from depreciating assets like factory equipment. Deductions based on lower, pre-inflation purchase prices effectively increased the tax burden.

Little wonder that tax shelters of just about every kind proliferated in the US during that period. Tax filers seeking to avoid increasing taxes and protect assets from inflation invested in everything from producing azaleas and almonds, to mink and trout farms. Movie production soared, as did the amount of vacant office space. All of this activity was not in response to real business opportunities, but for the express purpose of tax avoidance. Ever wonder why all those low-budget 1970s movies got made? With all this investment being wasted on dubious tax havens, no wonder the economy stalled.

## WHERE THIS LEADS: STAGFLATION

By favoring "market incumbents" over new ventures, directing capital into unproductive or protective investments instead of into growth-producing innovation—not to mention enabling government bloat—inflation slowly suffocates an economy.

**Fewer Start-ups, Abandoned Houses.** In the 1970s, investment in new ventures was devastated by murderous capital gains taxes and other inflated levies. Initial Public Offerings (IPOs) went from nearly $2 billion annually between 1969 to 1972 to a feeble $225 million between 1975 and 1978. The number of IPOs went from 1,026 in 1969 to a mere fifteen in 1975.

Things get even worse in countries with the highest levels of inflation. The small number of new ventures that do get off the ground often end up abandoned. That's why you see so many half-finished houses and office towers in countries that are chronic inflaters, like Venezuela and Peru.

Thanks to high inflation, Peruvians who started building new houses would run out of money and have to halt construction. In the 1990s, the Peruvian government tried to help people complete their houses by allowing them to stop paying property taxes. What happened? A fair number of Peruvians opted to live in partially constructed houses, which would allow them to forgo the taxes.

The story is similar in Venezuela, where the foremost inflation icon is the forty-five-story Torre de David (Tower of David). Intended to be the pride of Caracas, construction of the giant office building, which included a heliport, was halted in 1994. The building was taken over by around 1,000 indigent families, who camped out for years despite the lack of elevators. The Torre de David gained international notoriety as the world's tallest slum and has been the subject of television programs and documentaries.

Eventually the squatters were removed. The building today stands empty.

## THE SLOW STAGNATION OF
## "LOW-LEVEL INFLATION"

The lower levels of inflation experienced by the US during the past several decades have not produced this kind of disintegration. But they have caused a slow erosion of economic growth that may be the reason many people complain that "they can't get ahead."

During the gold standard years between 1950 and 1970, real GDP per capita grew by an annual rate of 2.77 percent. But over the past five decades, with a slowly declining fiat dollar, this growth rate has dropped significantly to 1.71 percent.

**What If We Had No Inflation?** The answer is that we'd be a lot wealthier. If the nation had the same growth rate today as we did in the 1950s and 1960s, per capita income would be 72 percent higher. Americans would be paid in dollars with more spending power. The economy would be at least 50 percent bigger. Investment would have been directed at high-value opportunities, rather than being misdirected due to confused, tax-distorted capital markets. Americans would be producing $10 trillion more goods and services than we do today.

A dollar with no inflation would mean a larger tax base generating more money for government, lessening the need for higher taxation. Congress might even balance the budget, as it did several times in the stable money eras of the 1950s and '60s, and again briefly in the late 1990s.

According to the government, the average American is

more than twice as wealthy as in 1970. But this increased wealth partly reflects advancements in technology, such as higher living standards brought about by better cars and smart phones, and also the spread of two-earner families. Would average Americans complain about how difficult it is to get ahead, or live on a single income, if we had the same growth rates as in the 1950s and '60s?

## More Government = Less Freedom

Sooner or later, inflation leads to more government control. The scenario is fairly standard: central banks devalue money; prices shoot up. Governments look for ways to tamp down inflation by keeping people from spending. They also respond with price controls, capital controls, higher taxes. Governments grow larger and often impose more constraints. People lose their freedom, and worse.

In ancient Rome, the Emperor Diocletian attempted to halt the empire's rampant inflation by imposing price controls on "900 commodities, 130 different grades of labor and a number of freight rates;" in other words, just about everything. Those who violated his edict were sentenced to death.

In the 1970s, Richard Nixon responded to inflation with wage and price controls. The US today has yet to see such constraints with the return of inflation. But the Fed's inflationary expansion of the money supply is enabling ever larger, more bloated government bureaucracy, with ever more control over private enterprise and people's lives.

**The Rise of the Regulatory State.** The Manhattan Institute's James Copland has noted that, since the late 1970s, more than 200,000 new rules have been added to the Federal Register. He also points out, "more than 300,000 federal crimes are on the books, but 98 percent of these were never voted on by Congress." This is only the federal government, not the state governments.

The potential of this vast bureaucracy to encroach on fundamental rights was demonstrated during the pandemic when the Centers for Disease Control and Prevention issued orders prohibiting landlords from evicting tenants who had stopped paying rent. The CDC's "eviction moratoria" had little, if anything, to do with disease or public health. Its overreach was subsequently overturned by the Supreme Court. Many questioned what an unelected health bureaucracy was doing issuing "laws" that are normally enacted by Congress.

This facilitation of government bloat and power led, in 2021, to a serious push to substantially expand IRS authority. This included calls for monitoring the personal bank accounts of individuals, which was a violation of privacy and constitutional rights.

Noted technologist and author George Gilder warns that the Fed's "scandal of money,"—its money creation via zero-percent interest rate borrowing—threatens capitalism by directing money away from growth-creating ventures and into social welfare bureaucracies. Millions of Americans whose savings and retirement accounts are being eroded by inflation are being pushed, Gilder says, into "acute dependency on government programs such as Social Security, disability, Medicaid, and Medicare." Instead of a society based on enterprise and upward mobility, the Fed's "scandal of money," Gilder says, is creating government dependency that is negating the American dream.

## TRUST UNRAVELS

But inflation's most damaging effect may be its debasement of social behavior. Money, after all, is more than a measuring instrument. By providing a mutually agreed-upon, stable unit of value, money facilitates trust between buyer and seller, lender and borrower. It helps people cooperate in a market economy based on expectations that promises will be fulfilled. *Money I'm borrowing from you will be the same value as the money I will use to repay you ten years from now.* Stable money promotes the market equivalent of the Golden Rule: do unto others as you would have them do unto you.

When money is no longer a trustworthy measure of value, these promises aren't kept. Market behavior and relationships between people become warped and distorted. Agreements are voided. Creditors lose their shirts. Debtors gain unexpected windfalls. Real wages decline. Pensioners find their monthly payments are inadequate. People are taxed unfairly.

Worst of all, no one knows why all of this is happening. You're not sure why prices are rising or why your money doesn't go as far as it once did. Meanwhile, you see certain people reaping unfair windfalls. They're getting rich not through honest work, but from distorted capital markets or government cronyism. Inflation, thus, foments a sense of unfairness and grievance. As John Maynard Keynes himself acknowledged: "There is no subtler, no surer means of overturning the existing basis of society than to debauch the currency."

At all levels of inflation, there is an undermining of social trust. Political divisions are inflamed. Angered by the unfairness and inequality they see around them people search for scapegoats.

The Romans in the third century blamed the Christians for the inflation caused by their own ruthless debasement of the denarius. Great Britain's witch trials in the sixteenth and seventeenth centuries, and the French Revolution's Reign of Terror in which 17,000 people were slaughtered, both coincided with periods of monetary chaos.

Finance, and people associated with it, are often demonized. During the Weimar hyperinflation, Germans blamed Jewish bankers. Nixon blamed "speculators" for a plunging US dollar. A few years later, he was blaming Arabs and "limits to growth."

In the aftermath of the financial crisis, the Fed's massive monetary "stimulus," (its expansion of the money supply via Quantitative Easing) helped trigger Occupy Wall Street demonstrations against "the rich" and "the 1 percent." That unrest, in various forms, continues today.

The late Nobel prize-winning Bulgarian writer Elias Canetti, who wrote about the social malaise that followed Germany's monetary collapse, provides an intriguing explanation for this characteristic reaction to inflation. Humiliated by the devaluation of their wealth, people retaliate by devaluing others. In his words: "Something must be treated in such a way that it becomes worth less and less, as the unit of money did during the inflation."

## Society Debased

If inflation hangs around long enough, and becomes severe enough, it becomes a truly vicious cycle. The economy deteriorates. The real value of tax revenues declines. People made poorer by inflation are paying less in real terms. The legitimacy of government collapses in a hyperinflation. Citizens resentful of higher taxes feel no moral imperative to pay them. Tax evasion soars. All of this just increases the pressure on government finances, leading to more money printing.

With this moral unraveling comes endless corruption. In Argentina, daily life means coping with constant disruption and turmoil. A resident writes that wage contracts can include several increases per year. There are constant labor strikes.

> Getting ahead seems impossible. Every day is a battle in Argentina, from hustling between stores comparing prices, to peso-pinching, to waiting in bank lines to pay bills or collect subsidies. So, they hunker down, try to survive, and resign themselves to the truth that there is no "Argentine Dream."

It's no accident, he suggests, that the country has the most psychologists per capita. Corruption is rampant. With so much power concentrated in the hands of oligarchs and bureaucrats, pay-offs and kick-backs are a part of doing business.

**Morality Corrupted.** Inflation severs the link between effort and reward. Adam Fergusson writes that in Weimar Germany, "As the old virtues of thrift, honesty and hard work lost their appeal, everybody was out to get rich quickly, especially as speculation in currency or shares could palpably yield far greater rewards than labour." Before World War I, bribery had been almost unheard of. However, by 1924,

> There were few in any class of society who were not infected by, or prey to, the pervasive, soul-destroying influence

of the constant erosion of capital or earnings and uncertainty about the future. From tax-evasion, food-hoarding, currency speculation, or illegal exchange transactions—all crimes against the State, each of which to a greater or lesser degree became for individuals a matter of survival—it was a short step to breaching one or other of the Ten Commandments.

Crime soars in nations with rampant inflation. Brazil, a chronic inflater, has long been bedeviled by rampant crime and by lawless police behavior. Hyperinflater Venezuela, where the annual inflation rate has been as high as 60,000 percent, has the highest crime rate of any nation in South America.

Studies have shown that inflation can have a stronger connection to crime than unemployment. Richard Rosenfeld, Curators' Professor of Criminology and Criminal Justice at the University of Missouri–St. Louis, has noted that, "A key mechanism linking inflation to crime is the price of stolen goods." He explains, "Price increases make cheap, stolen goods more attractive and therefore strengthen incentives for those who supply the underground markets with stolen goods. The reverse occurs when inflation is low."

## ARE WE ROME?

When we think of worst-case scenarios of extreme inflation we usually think of the fall of Rome and the Great Disorder of post-World War I Weimar Germany. Largely overlooked is the role that currency devaluations have played in just about every major societal upheaval.

Radical inflation has inflamed tensions not only in Venezuela and Argentina, but also in countries throughout the Middle East. The 2010 Tunisian street demonstrations that set off the Arab Spring protests were largely over food prices. The unrest then spilled over into Egypt, where the consumer price index had jumped to 18 percent by 2008. That led to the toppling of President Mubarak's administration, and later, that of his successor, President Morsi. Unrest also increased in Iran, where inflation surged to an official rate of 25 percent in 2008. It has since gone far higher.

In 1989, a hyperinflation began in Russia that took the ruble from four per dollar on the black market to roughly 5,000 per dollar. In 1991, the Soviet Union splintered, and civil war erupted in Chechnya. Indonesia suffered price rises of 40 percent annually after a currency disaster in 1997, and East Timor decided to secede. In the 1980s, Yugoslavia suffered a hyperinflation that eventually led to its breakup into six countries: Serbia, Croatia, Slovenia, Montenegro, Bosnia, and North Macedonia.

**Dictators Rise Up.** What happens when you get this kind of unrest? People often turn to strongmen and dictators. In the 1790s, a hyperinflation in revolutionary France led to the eventual rise of Napoleon, who stabilized the currency by linking it to gold. In the early twentieth century, the post-World War I inflation that rolled through many European nations helped set the stage for the rise of not only Adolf Hitler but the other dictators of the interwar period: Benito Mussolini in Italy, Francisco Franco in Spain, Miklos Horthy of Hungary, and Joseph Stalin in Russia.

## THE DANGER NO ONE IS WORRYING ABOUT, YET

In a candid interview before the COVID pandemic and shortly before his death, former Fed Chair Paul Volcker warned of the dangers of monetary policy that aimed to create 2 percent inflation. "Once you begin aiming at 2 percent, then you hear people say, 'Well, maybe we can give the economy a little more juice by going to 3 percent.' Well, if that doesn't work, we'll go to 4 percent." This is one reason that, he said, "inflation finally feeds upon itself when it gets going."

By late 2021, Volcker's prediction had come true. Inflation exceeded 6 percent. The US is not Weimar Germany, nor for that matter Argentina or Venezuela. But the low-level inflation of the past two decades has been damaging. It has resulted in a 38 percent erosion of the dollar's purchasing power, an inflationary housing bubble that exploded into a global financial crisis, the severest recession since the Great Depression, and violent unrest not seen in decades.

Studies have shown that trust in American political institutions has plunged since the relatively stable money era of the 1990s. Politics has become more polarized than at any other time in recent memory. Street violence has erupted not only in the US but in nations around the world. Radical movements are flouting social norms and attacking the fundamental values and symbols of America's system of democratic capitalism, including the Constitution and the Founding Fathers. Government has grown larger and more intrusive; political rhetoric darker and more pessimistic.

The rise of social media and the COVID pandemic did play a role in these events. Yet the frequent demonizing and scapegoating we hear in public discourse increasingly has the feel of the nation in the grip of an inflationary malaise. An example: the Biden administration blaming meat producers and other industries for high prices and "profiteering."

Inflation's debasement of US society is not just a domestic issue. By undermining the entrepreneurial dynamism that has long been the source of our nation's strength, inflation threatens our national security. We saw this begin to play out in the 1970s. Inflation had weakened the nation's economy and sapped its political will. The US retreated from Southeast Asia and abandoned the South Vietnamese. Cuba's Soviet-style communism seemed poised to take over Central America. Nicaragua aligned itself with Havana and Moscow. There was a perception of America in decline. The nation's military became neglected. Naval vessels fell into disrepair. Weakness emboldened our adversaries. Russia felt free to march into Afghanistan in December 1979. The US was unable to rescue diplomats taken hostage by Iran.

Fortunately, by the early 1980s, stagflation was extinguished. America's strength was restored during the administration of Ronald Reagan. As we will see in the next chapter, he was one of a select group of leaders who successfully defeated a major inflation.

## CHAPTER FOUR

# How to End the Malaise

H OW DO COUNTRIES control inflation? The answer is: *very badly.* The misunderstanding of money that leads governments and central banks to devalue currency too often means they're ill-equipped to put the Inflation Genie back in the bottle. History is littered with attempts to end monetary disasters that have failed and frequently made things worse.

This is because policymakers are usually unable, or unwilling, to acknowledge the real reasons why their currency has lost value. Instead, they blame markets: People are spending too much money! Businesses are gouging! The economy is overheating! Do something!

Often, that something is pressuring businesses to lower prices, or getting people to spend less money. These strategies never work.

**Argentina: Capital Controls Fail.** Many countries attempt to shore up their plunging currency by artificially increasing demand for it through so-called "capital controls." Argentina has periodically restricted companies from doing business in dollars in an attempt to shore up its beleaguered peso. The use of credit cards has been limited, too. These controls have decimated Argentine trade, which is largely conducted in dollars. They were lifted for a while, then reimposed again. In 2021, after a brief dip, Argentina's inflation (which had reached rates of 50 percent) was once again soaring. The value of the Argentine peso had fallen from 15 to the dollar in 2017 to 107 to the dollar.

**Turkey: Cracking Down on "Food Terrorists."** Price controls are another favorite method, often accompanied by threats and shaming from authoritarian regimes. Turkey's strongman President Recep Tayyip Erdogan responded to rising food prices resulting from a sliding Turkish lira by blaming foreign "food terrorists" he claimed were working with international speculators. He called on citizens to report food sellers who were "bullying" consumers, and ordered price inspections of food shops and warehouses. To provide some price competition, the government also opened stalls to sell discounted food and other products. The efforts have had virtually no effect on Turkey's skyrocketing inflation. Food prices continue to rise by more than 25 percent annually.

**Venezuela: More Money Printing.** With an inflation rate that's the highest in the world, Venezuela at one point imposed tight price controls on everything from corn flour and car parts, to children's toys. The government sent a small army of price inspectors armed with central bank data in pursuit of supposed price gougers. After further devastating the nation's economy, the controls were eventually relaxed. Meanwhile, the government keeps printing money to help fund its soaring salaries, which went up at least sixty-fold in one year alone.

**The Nixon Shock: Prices Explode.** Price controls were also a favorite method of the thirty-seventh president of the United States. Facing a mild inflation in 1971, Richard Nixon responded with a ninety-day freeze on wages and prices—the only peacetime wage and price controls in US history. He later instituted a Pay Board and Price Commission that was to approve wage and price increases. Nixon was convinced that the controls, combined with the Fed's monetary expansion, would boost employment with minimal inflation. The president did win reelection, but his initiatives did anything but tame price increases. After the greenback's link to gold was severed, its value plummeted on the foreign exchanges, sending the CPI rocketing into the stratosphere.

Over the next four years, the annual rate of inflation reached double digits. After Nixon was forced to resign from office, his successor, Gerald Ford, responded to upwardly spiraling oil prices in 1974 with a PR campaign that distributed big red buttons with the acronym "WIN," which stood for Whip Inflation Now! (See page 42.) The campaign included a call to action that encouraged things like carpooling, turning down thermostats, and starting vegetable gardens.

Inflation was temporarily curtailed by a brutal recession with high unemployment. The WIN campaign, however, did little to halt the dollar's slide, which later resumed. The buttons ended up as collectors' items, available on eBay and remembered in history books as symbols of an administration's feckless response to inflation.

Gerald Ford's successor, President Jimmy Carter, tried to reduce oil price inflation by buying less foreign oil, yet that only lengthened what were by then called "Carter gas lines." In a famous speech, while wearing a cardigan sweater, he implored citizens to lower their thermostats. The request did little to cool the inflation rate, which reached nearly 15 percent by the end of his term.

## The Myth of Inflation Fighting Through "Austerity"

Another inflation-fighting strategy is "austerity," a combination of harsh tax increases, super-high interest rates, government spending cuts and, yes, more currency devaluation. These so-called remedies are based on a flawed critique of the Great Depression. Back then (and, too often, today) Keynesians saw inflation as primarily a non-monetary phenomenon. They attributed it to too much demand for goods and services from a booming economy. In other words, they blamed it on *prosperity*. Deflation, they believed, came from an economic bust. The objective of austerity measures is to tamp down inflationary price increases by creating a "recession to break the back of inflation."

That's not the only head-scratcher behind these draconian initiatives. Proponents claim those severe tax hikes are "good" because they'll ostensibly help governments balance budgets and avoid having to print money. They'll also "cool consumer demand," which will lessen pressure on prices.

Equally improbable are the justifications for austerity's

super-high interest rates, which can hit levels of 15 percent or much higher. They're supposedly needed to bring on that much-needed recession. The high rates are also intended to attract investment in a country's high-yielding securities. Since investors would presumably have to use the nation's money to buy its bonds, austerity advocates maintain that raising rates increases demand for that currency and, thus, its value. At least, that's the thinking.

Austerity is a favorite inflation-fighting "remedy" of the International Monetary Fund (IMF), the global organization of 190 countries whose mission, in part, is to foster global financial stability. Nations plagued by severe inflation often turn to IMF experts. They shouldn't. States around the world have seen their crises worsened and their economies devastated after taking the agency's advice. Why do so many nations keep listening? Because those that do are rewarded by rich aid packages that can bring in hundreds of millions, if not billions, of dollars—money that often ends up in private bank accounts of government officials.

**The IMF's Bad Medicine in Asia.** The classic example of IMF malpractice was its intervention in the Asian currency crisis in the late 1990s. As the dollar rose during that time, it put pressure on the values of dollar-linked currencies in Asia. Traders dropped the Thai baht and other currencies in the region, and instead bought dollars.

The IMF, however, insisted the problem lay with the Thai government's deficit. The agency recommended an austerity program of tax hikes and spending restrictions to turn the government's tiny deficit into a surplus. The strategy, however, was a disaster. The value of the baht fell further.

Demonstrations broke out over increased taxes on petroleum products. Eventually, Thailand reversed these policies and the baht began to recover.

**A Russian Currency Disaster.** In the late 1980s and early 1990s, Russia made a similar mistake of consulting the IMF when facing a spiraling inflation caused by the collapse of the ruble. Demand for the ruble plummeted as Russia began to conduct more international trade in US dollars as part of President Mikhail Gorbachev's "Perestroika" policy of warmer relations with the West. At the same time, Russia's bureaucratic Communist government began to finance its enormous deficits by printing new banknotes. The combined result was a roaring hyperinflation.

Russia's IMF advisers recommended slowing the hyperinflation by reducing the supply of rubles. Citizens were ordered to turn in their higher denominated notes for a similar amount in smaller denominations, but with a kicker: citizens were allowed to exchange a maximum of only 1,000 rubles per person. The government effectively stole money from beleaguered Russian citizens. The problem, however, was not supply per se, but that no one trusted the ruble. By declaring a huge swath of its currency worthless, Russia made this problem exponentially worse. Why would you hold rubles? The ruble collapsed on world currency markets. Russia's industrial production and GDP fell.

By this time, Gorbachev had been succeeded by Boris Yeltsin, who undertook reforms to privatize Russia's state-run economy. Prices for many other goods, such as petroleum, were also liberalized, and taxes were raised even further. There was no transition to a genuine market economy.

Crushed by hyperinflation and impossible taxes, the economy fell to pieces.

What emerged, instead, was economic chaos. The ruble was essentially valueless. Factories that were still functioning were using their own products to pay employees. Workers would receive crates of toilet paper, brake pads, or mattresses, which they would then sell on the black market, thus evading Russia's loathed Value Added Tax. Russian agriculture turned inward. Workers ate what they grew. City dwellers started their own gardens in backyards and on rooftops to ensure a steady supply of calories.

To stem the devastation, the IMF then recommended—and Russia imposed—a round of austerity that included a raft of new taxes in addition to spending reductions, with the goal of creating a fiscal surplus. The tax hikes simply accelerated the downward pressure on the ruble. The IMF-created disaster led to the election of strongman Vladimir Putin.

## WHY THE "FIXES" FAIL

Inflation-fighting regulations and taxes fail because they don't properly address the cause of a crisis—a decline in the value of money. The failure to address this central problem produces "solutions" that, in one way or another, further undermine confidence in a government and its currency, making matters worse.

**The Problem with Price Controls.** Wage and price controls are essentially "inflation in reverse." They result in prices that are artificially low. A frequent consequence is shortages. Hence those 1970s gas lines or those empty store shelves in Russia, Venezuela, and other nations that have imposed such constraints.

**Currency Controls Create Black Markets.** Regulations forcing citizens to use a nation's near-worthless money can boost demand and improve currency values—at least initially. Malaysia and China were able to weather the Asian crises with the help of currency controls. But they only work as a stopgap measure. People find ways around them. Argentinians restricted from using dollars circumvent controls via black markets. Black-market currency traders known as *arbolitos* ("little trees") have been a part of life for decades, shouting *Cambio! Cambio!* ("change") to passersby on the street. Tourists can get a favorable rate selling their dollars, which the *arbolitos* then sell to inflation-weary Argentinians.

**What's Wrong With "Austerity?"** Like all the other policy misfires, austerity's focus on suppressing prices by creating a recession totally misses the point that inflation is fundamentally not about prices rising from too much consumption, but about a drop in a nation's currency value. As we saw with IMF interventions in Asia and Russia, austerity's harsh measures may be good at bringing on a recession. But they usually don't end inflation and more often exacerbate a crisis. High taxes kill economic activity, and those super-high interest rates don't attract investors. No interest rate is high enough to create an appetite for an unreliable currency. Instead, commerce slumps. Demand for money is destroyed, perpetuating an oversupply. Inflation rages on.

Imagine what would happen in the United States if the Fed

suddenly targeted an overnight Fed funds rate of 25 percent. No one could afford to borrow. Investment would be stopped cold. The carnage in the stock market would be spectacular. The dollar would almost certainly tank as a result.

Yes, austerity brings on recession. But the strategy is a little like the old-time medical practice of bloodletting to cure disease. The disease is "cured," but the patient dies.

**Foreign Exchange Intervention.** Central banks will also turn to the additional austerity measure of attempting to support currency values by using their reserves of foreign currencies—say, dollars or euros—to buy up their own currency on the foreign exchange market. If you've read up to this point, you might think this would work. After all, aren't they reducing an oversupply of money? But such "foreign exchange interventions," as they're called, often fail. Why? Because, after a central bank buys up its own currency, it ends up dumping it back into the domestic economy. There's no reduction in the money supply. In central-banker terminology, such foreign exchange interventions end up "sterilized." When the market sees central banks doing this, it knows that failure is likely. Confidence falls further. Both Thailand and Indonesia made this mistake during the 1990s Asian crisis and failed to halt their inflations.

**The IMF's "One-Size-Fits-All" Solutions.** Not all inflations, as we've noted, are the result of government deficits and an expanding money supply. In the Asian crisis, many of the troubled countries had some of the cleanest government accounts in the world, certainly far superior than most developed countries. Thailand and South Korea, to cite just two examples, had government debts of less than 10 percent of gross domestic product in 1996. Yet this reality was lost on IMF bureaucrats whose top-down recommendations totally misfired.

**A Tangle of Strings Attached.** The IMF's recommendations also come with a fair dose of politics. IMF loans are intended to help get a nation back on its feet and boost confidence in a nation's currency. But they can come with countless requirements that reflect the wish-lists of politicians.

That was the case with Indonesia, another nation whose currency took a dive during the Asian crisis. Reformers within the Indonesian government gleefully added their own pet projects to the IMF's list of loan conditions. Conservatives wanted various free-market reforms. Liberals wanted human rights and environmental regulations that included, yes, restrictions on fishing.

None of the IMF's 100-plus conditions for lending did anything to boost the value of Indonesia's currency, the rupiah, and solve the country's monetary crisis. The only thing that did work, temporarily, was a proposal to establish a currency board on the advice of noted Johns Hopkins University economist Steve Hanke. Currency boards link a nation's currency to the more stable currency of another nation. They're a surefire way to fix hyperinflation. Yet the IMF, with help from President Bill Clinton, ultimately pressured Indonesia's President Suharto to abandon the program. What happened? The rupiah collapsed again. Jakarta was rocked by riots and Suharto eventually had to step down.

The IMF's packages of loans don't compensate for its often-toxic prescriptions. The IMF has loaned hundreds of millions of dollars in aid to Zimbabwe. Yet that country has failed to stop its notorious hyperinflation. Things got so bad that the nation more than once had to actually throw out its currency and start over, which hasn't helped either.

## HOW TO *REALLY* FIX INFLATION

How do you end inflation? The good news is that a nation doesn't need tax hikes, super-high interest rates, horrible recessions—or even fishing restrictions. The way to do it, very simply, is to stabilize the value of money.

How to achieve this? When a currency begins to slide, the first step should be for a government to publicly declare its intention to support its money, i.e., maintain its value. The way to do so is, very simply, by shrinking the monetary base. (Remember, currency loses value when there's an oversupply in relation to demand.) As people realize that the central bank is dealing with the crisis, demand for the currency, and hence its worth, will swiftly increase. Investors relish the prospect of being paid returns in sound money. Confidence rises. The currency rebounds, and the economy picks up. A central bank might soon have to meet the surging demand by increasing the money supply just to keep the currency from rising too much!

There are two basic ways to reduce the base money supply. One is through an intervention whereby a government buys its own currency in the foreign exchange markets. Didn't we just say that these maneuvers generally fail? That's because nations don't carry them out properly. A foreign exchange intervention *will* work if the transaction results in a net reduction of the money supply. Central banks must not make the all-too-common mistake of plowing the currency they acquire back into their domestic economy, a process known as "sterilization." For every dollar or euro used in a foreign exchange transaction, the money supply must *shrink* by the same amount.

The other method is selling assets, typically government bonds, in exchange for the domestic currency—in other words, open market operations. Currency is received in payment, which shrinks the money supply.

A final way back to a healthy currency, as we'll see below, is through enacting pro-market policies. An expanding economy with an appetite for money tends to mean more currency demand, which encourages higher values. There's less pressure on central banks to stimulate a weak economy with "easy money."

## Money Miracles in Postwar Germany and Japan

In the immediate aftermath of World War II until 1949, Germany again suffered from hyperinflation as banknotes were printed to fund government deficits. By one estimate, as many as half of all transactions took place through barter. Cigarettes and chocolate circulated as money.

**Sound Money and Regulatory Decontrol End Germany's Post-War Inflation.** The Allied powers stepped in and invited a Detroit-based banker, Joseph Dodge, to fix Germany's hyperinflation. He immediately outlawed deficit spending by the government. The government could not spend money unless it first received revenue from taxes. This relieved pressure on the central bank to finance the government. The hyperinflated Reichsmark was replaced by a new currency, the Deutsche Mark, which was linked to the gold-based US dollar. The terrible inflation ended overnight.

Germany's newly appointed director of the Office of Economic Opportunity, Ludwig Erhard, took the opposite of the austerity approach. He paired the newly reliable Deutsche Mark, which he had helped create, with big tax cuts. He also lifted all kinds of wage and price controls, and ended rationing that had been put in place during the war. The German economy soared. Erhard subsequently became economics minister of the newly formed Federal Republic of Germany and later its chancellor, implementing a series of tax cuts. The top income tax rate fell from 95 percent to 53 percent, while the income at which the top rate applied rose from 60,000 marks to 110,040 marks. Germany's economy became one of the world's strongest during the 1950s and 1960s. With a booming economy, there was no pressure on the central bank to get the economy going with "easy money." The German mark became one of the most reliable currencies in the world, and eventually served as the core of the euro.

**Japan: A Government Spending Ban and a Yen Linked to the Dollar.** Fresh from his success in Germany, Joseph Dodge was then sent to Tokyo to work the same magic. There, too, the central bank was printing money to fund the government. Hyperinflation ravaged the economy. Dodge again imposed a strict ban on deficit spending, which lasted until 1965, and linked the Japanese yen to the gold-backed dollar.

The crisis ended instantly. But this was not austerity. Like Germany, Japan reduced its taxes dramatically. The national sales tax was eliminated. In a series of tax reductions in the 1950s, the top income tax rate fell from 85 percent to 55 percent. Dividends, interest income, and capital gains had been taxed at regular income-tax rates. Soon, dividends were taxed at a lower rate; interest income was taxed at only 10 percent; and capital gains were tax-free. The country achieved growth rates comparable to those of present-day China and became one of the premier world economies. Its "economic miracle" eventually surpassed Germany's.

Both countries demonstrated the effectiveness of what co-author Nathan Lewis calls "The Magic Formula:" sound money and low taxes.

## How Paul Volcker Whipped the 1970s Stagflation

Thirty years later, the US faced a different challenge during the 1970s. Prices were soaring after Richard Nixon had taken the dollar off gold, its traditional anchor of value. By the end of the decade, inflation had reached nearly 15 percent. The US had become so mired in "stagflation" that inflationary expectations had taken hold. Ever-rising prices were seen as part of the natural order.

Enter Paul Volcker, who became chair of the Federal Reserve during the Carter administration, in August 1979. By then, central bank "easy money" was finally acknowledged as the cause of the sick economy. Volcker had a mandate to fix the problem. But his initial efforts were a failure. Volcker started out with a "monetarist experiment" that narrowly focused on adjusting the money supply, without direct attention to the value of the currency.

This strategy, however, didn't work. One reason is that the Federal Reserve can directly control only a portion of the total money supply. The central bank controls so-called "base money," which is the amount of currency in circulation and in bank reserves. It does not manage things like checking accounts, certificates of deposit, or money market funds. Yet such "near cash" instruments have a direct impact on economic activity and inflation. Volcker's monetarist approach also paid no attention to currency values. The effort, therefore, misfired. The result was a rollercoaster—a sickening collapse in the value of the dollar, as reflected in the gold price which shot up from around $300 per ounce of gold to $850 per ounce five months later.

Not long afterwards, the dollar rebounded. But the CPI was still rising. Volcker became convinced that the monetarist approach wasn't working. The only way to cure the malaise was through harsh austerity, including allowing interest rates to reach unprecedented levels. Yet, as we've previously noted, measures like the CPI can be slow to reflect moves by the Fed. So Volcker once again miscalculated. By 1982, the gold price had fallen back to $300 an ounce—a doubling in the dollar's value since Reagan's inauguration.

This tightening had produced the desired recession. Prices were coming down. But, as Volcker acknowledged, he may have gone too far. "Interest rates went way up above our expectations." The rate for a four-year mortgage was more than 18 percent; the best short-term lending rate was more than 21 percent. The cost was a painful downturn. Unemployment reached a level that exceeded the high of the 2008-09 economic crisis. Plunging commodities prices devastated farmers, who drove their tractors to the Federal Reserve headquarters in protest. Homebuilders mailed bricks and wooden planks to the Fed. Auto dealers sent the keys of cars that went unsold.

In hindsight, it's easy to say that Volcker should have taken his foot off the brake sooner. But he was likely haunted by the repeated failures of his predecessors. Past attempts had produced pauses, only to see inflation return and prices soar ever higher. Americans were desperate for a solution. Volcker had to make certain that, this time, the inflation beast was not coming back.

He finally abandoned his harsh methods when he realized that the ever-strengthening dollar was in danger of triggering a global financial crisis. The rise in the greenback's value meant that the debt burdens for nations borrowing in US dollars had effectively doubled. Mexico let it be known that it might default. Since American banks held considerable amounts of Latin American debt, the meltdown could spread to the US. To head off such a calamity, Volcker started loosening to get more liquidity into the banking system. The over-tightening and the deflation ended. Interest rates plummeted and the stock market soared.

Thereafter, Volcker tracked gold and commodity prices in an effort to keep the dollar stable. He was now focusing on the value of the currency, rather than on money supply statistics alone. Volcker's success, combined with Ronald Reagan's free-market policies, set off an economic boom. After an initial recession in the early 1980s, the US economy grew by 4.3 percent per year between 1983 and 1989. The Misery Index—a measure that combines unemployment and inflation rates—dropped from 22 percent, its high during the Carter years, to 7 percent by the end of 1986.

Paul Volcker's loose commodity standard was not as effective as a traditional gold standard. The dollar still fluctuated wildly between $300 and $500 per ounce of gold. Alan Greenspan succeeded Volcker as Fed Chair in 1987. A longtime advocate of a return to the gold standard, he refined Volcker's strategy, taming the volatility of the dollar still further and keeping it closer to $350 per ounce.

**"The Great Moderation."** Greenspan later acknowledged that his policy at the time was to maintain a stable dollar through what was essentially a *de facto* gold standard. He explained in a 2004 Congressional testimony, "[The] most effective central banks in this fiat money period tend to be successful largely because we tend to replicate [that] which would probably have occurred under a commodity standard."

Central banks around the world followed Greenspan's approach. "Since the late '70s, central bankers generally have behaved as though we were on the gold standard," he said in 2005. Greenspan's policy of currency stability provided the foundation of the "Great Moderation," the low-inflation, high-growth era of the 1980s and 1990s. His achievement won accolades, including a reverential nickname, "the Maestro," and a knighthood. Unfortunately, in the late 1990s, Greenspan ignored the signals of gold and commodities, and allowed the dollar's value to rise to painful levels. The strong dollar set off the Asian monetary crisis.

To this day, most economists still don't understand that the critical factor in the 1970s stagflation, as well as in the Great Moderation of the 1980s and '90s, was the value of the dollar.

**Russia: An Unlikely Success Story.** The IMF's disastrous program in Russia in the late 1990s set the stage for Vladimir Putin, who rose to power on the promise that he could end the devastating hyperinflation that had reduced Russia to a barter economy. His optimistic vision of 7 percent growth rates was readily embraced by a country that had spent the previous two decades in disarray.

Shortly after entering office in August 1999, Putin almost immediately delivered. A long list of taxes was lowered or discarded. In 2000, he passed a radical 13 percent flat income tax, the lowest in the world. The flat tax had the additional advantage of being inflation-proof. There were no tax brackets and thus no "bracket creep." As businesses geared up for a boom, demand for the ruble naturally increased, allowing it to stabilize at around 29 per dollar.

The result: the Russian economy grew 10 percent in 2000, the first year of high growth since the 1960s. Thanks to the new 13 percent flat tax, income tax revenues rose 46 percent in a single year. No longer was there any reason to evade taxes. With reduced levies and a reliable currency, Russia's resurgence echoed that of Germany's in the 1950s. Unfortunately, this amazing economic expansion was halted by the worldwide financial crisis of 2008. In the recession that ensued, taxes were raised dramatically and the ruble fell to pieces. Russia's central bank had responded with an austerity strategy of ultra-high interest rates of more than 30 percent. Yet predictably, this failed to subdue inflation. Writing in the Russian online magazine Pravda.ru, co-author Nathan Lewis recommended that the country's central bank shore up the ruble with an "unsterilized" foreign exchange intervention to reduce the monetary base. This prescription was followed in February 2009 and was an immediate success. The ruble's value soared. Interest rates plummeted to less than 10 percent a few months later. Russia's crisis had ended.

## WHAT NOW?

What about the US? Can America tame its increasing inflation? The answer is that we can, and we can do so quickly. The financial stability and the vibrant growth of the 1980s and '90s is possible once again if the US reawakens to the importance of a sound dollar, and has the political will to keep its value stable. Below, we describe several ways how the US, or other countries, can put an end to inflation.

**Currency Boards.** We explained earlier that a currency board is a monetary authority that operates much like a gold-standard system. But, instead of linking a currency to gold, it is linked to the dollar, euro, or another more stable "anchor" currency. Currency boards have been around for more than 150 years. They've achieved miraculous success in halting even the most violent hyperinflations, often in a matter of days. They can't lend or print money and have none of the powers of central banks. Their sole mission is to prevent inflation by making sure money maintains a fixed value.

Johns Hopkins economist Steve Hanke, who has helped design currency boards for nations around the world, explains a local currency is backed "100 percent" by an anchor currency to boost confidence. "If you don't like the local currency that's being issued by the Currency Board, you [can] exchange it for the anchor currency," he says. "And there's always anchor currency because of the 100 percent reserve requirement."

Two Baltic states, Lithuania and Estonia, stopped terrible inflations in the 1990s by instituting this system. Latvia achieved the same result with a quasi-currency board. All three survived the 2008 financial crisis without currency turmoil, while other regional currencies plummeted. A number of countries in Africa also use currency board-like systems. These monetary authorities all use the euro as their anchor currency. Hong Kong has had a currency board tied to the dollar since 1983.

In 1997, Hanke advised the government of Bulgaria to adopt this solution to restore confidence in its currency, the lev, and end a vicious hyperinflation with an annual rate at one point surpassing 2,000 percent. On Hanke's advice, Bulgaria's ailing money was fixed to Germany's and "magically, the lev became a clone of the mighty German mark." What happened next? "Almost within twenty-four hours," he recounts, "inflation [was] wiped out of the system. And, in a month, nominal interest rates in Bulgaria were in single digits." Bulgaria's economy, which had been contracting by more than 10 percent annually, abruptly turned around and was soon growing at a robust rate of nearly 5 percent.

Examples like that of Bulgaria, and other countries that have used currency boards, demonstrate that if the currency's value is stabilized—i.e., linked to the dollar or the euro—even the most extreme hyperinflation will end.

Hanke has noted that some seventy currency boards have been used around the world. "There has never been one that has failed." But he emphasizes that it's important that a currency board system follows the rules. Argentina set up a "convertibility system" in early 1991 that has been mistakenly called a currency board. It didn't work because it operated more like a central bank, engaging in money creation that undermined the link between the Argentine peso and its anchor currency, the dollar.

The success of currency boards points up the importance of stable money to taming inflation. In Hanke's words: "Stability might not be everything, but everything is nothing without stability."

**A Commodities Standard.** Another effective method is the

Volcker-Greenspan strategy that relies on commodities and gold prices as barometers of the dollar's value. When their prices rise, that means the dollar is slipping and it's time to tighten the supply of base money. Commodities and gold prices falling? Time to expand the supply of base money. As Alan Greenspan acknowledged, this system is an imperfect approximation of a gold standard. That begs the question: Why not use the real thing?

## The Absolute Best Way to End Inflation

By far, the best way to stabilize the dollar is to return to the system that worked for most of our history, that was the foundation of America's storied prosperity—a gold-standard system.

With a gold standard, there would be no inflation. There was no inflation during the gold standard era in the late nineteenth century, an age of historic wealth creation that, in many respects, has yet to be equaled even today.

*No inflation*, however, does not necessarily mean an end to fluctuating prices. Prices, as we've explained elsewhere, will continue to rise and fall in response to changes in supply, demand, and productivity. A gold-pegged dollar, however, would remove the price distortion that occurs with any level of inflation. It would allow prices to convey real market values. In other words, gold would enable money, for the first time in decades, to completely fulfill its role as a measure of worth and a facilitator of transactions. People conducting business in the marketplace would have a tool that really works. Commerce would boom.

A gold standard would not only eliminate inflation. Studies have shown that the number of major financial crises have dramatically risen in the fiat-money era since 1971. No economic crisis was ever caused by stable money.

The connection between sound money and a prosperous economy has been demonstrated repeatedly. This is illustrated not only by the historic wealth creation of the nineteenth century, but also the industrious, post-war years of the 1950s and '60s, when the world was on the Bretton Woods gold standard. In the words of economist Judy Shelton: "We had maximum shared growth. It wasn't just the wealthiest at the expense of the poorest. It was shared. Everybody was moving up [...] All around the world, you had these fantastic economic performance indicators and it is amazing to me that people don't see that this era of fantastic growth, productive growth, shared growth, coincided, perfectly, with the era during which the world had a fixed exchange rate system."

## GOLD: THE WAY FORWARD

So how do we get there from here? A return to a world of zero inflation and sound money, achieved by a return to a gold standard, is entirely possible and far easier than many people think.

There are several different gold standard systems. Two have been put into practice. The first is the classical gold standard, which was used by the world's largest economies from 1870 to the outbreak of the First World War in 1914. The other is the gold exchange standard, which was used after both world wars. Another two have been proposed: a 100 percent gold-backed currency; and what we call the gold price system. Each has its critics and supporters. But in all of these systems, the value of currency is linked to gold, which is the anchor of value.

This is not at all a novel concept. Dozens of countries today link their currencies to the dollar or euro for the purpose of achieving stability. The US would simply be linking the dollar to the precious metal whose value, over centuries, has proven more stable than any currency. Below, we outline a proposal for a new gold standard that would work in the twenty-first century.

**A Twenty-First Century Gold Standard.** Our proposal combines the fundamentals of the old systems, while avoiding their vulnerabilities. The United States doesn't have to worry about stockpiles of gold. No need for those vaults with mountains of gold bars. All you have to do is keep the value of the currency linked to gold.

Under this system, the dollar would be fixed to gold at a particular price. That price might be decided based on a five- or ten-year average of recent gold prices, marked up as insurance against deflation. The Federal Reserve would use its tools, primarily open market operations, to keep the value of the dollar tied at that rate to gold. Just as currency boards do today, the supply of money would contract when the currency was a little weak and expand when the currency became too strong.

**Easy Implementation.** Implementing the program would take no more than twelve months. The government should announce a certain date when the conversion to a gold standard would take place. A gradual phase-in would help markets prepare for the return to gold-based money. During periods of weakening currency the price of gold reflects investors' fears. The announcement of a coming gold standard would help calm such anxieties. A more natural gold price should reemerge, making it easier to arrive at the gold/dollar ratio. The transition period would also enable financial institutions and investors to adjust expectations about future interest rates and alter investment strategies to reflect a new environment of stable money. Global markets would make similar adjustments. The dollar would be permitted to fluctuate against gold with a range of 1 percent, the rate used under the Bretton Woods system for currencies against the dollar.

**A Role for the Fed?** The Fed would lose its "dual mandate." No longer would the central bank be tasked with curing unemployment with "easy money" and interest-rate manipulation. Such efforts, as we've discussed, end up undermining growth and job creation. The Fed would not be in the business of fixing the federal funds rate, the interest rate banks pay when borrowing from each other. Nor could it pay interest on banks' reserves. The Fed could still set the discount rate that banks pay to borrow money from the Fed at its discount window. That charge would be set above free-market rates of similar maturities so that banks don't use the window to get a cheap source of money to lend out. This was the basic methodology of the Bank of England of the late nineteenth century, when the British pound was the world's premier gold-linked currency.

If the United States went to gold, other countries would likely fix their money to the dollar, if only for convenience. Numerous countries in Latin America and Asia already try to keep their currencies closely aligned to the greenback because doing so makes trading and investing with the United States much easier. Part of the task would be to make sure that their central banks understood how to defend their ties to the dollar and, therefore, avoid the kind of speculative attacks seen in the 1997 Asian crisis. This would mean encouraging them to link to the dollar (which many already have) or tie their money to gold directly. Either approach would achieve the main objective of a return to stable exchange rates and sound money.

## Getting Past Myths About Gold

Unlike Keynesian notions whose own advocates concede are "counterintuitive," the idea of vanquishing inflation and bringing about prosperity through sound money makes total sense. Unfortunately, for the last several decades, the economics profession has been captive to its own "cancel culture." Keynesians, who have long dominated the field, have shut down all discussion of a return to a gold standard.

Their rigid stance is partly due to their long-held misunderstanding of how a gold standard operates, as well as to human nature. With nothing to do but maintain the dollar's link to gold, the Federal Reserve would not need a staff of more than 20,000. John Maynard Keynes himself essentially admitted to the attraction of power that comes from managing—or more accurately, mismanaging—economies via the manipulation of floating fiat currencies.

Whatever the reasons, truly ending inflation will require overcoming resistance to the idea of a return to gold-based money. Below are some of the common raps on gold, which are easily answered.

**The Rap:** "Gold's price fluctuations mean that it's too 'volatile' to provide a stable anchor for the dollar."

**Answer:** Not true. The intrinsic value of gold doesn't change very much. Gold has provided a stable anchor for currencies for thousands of years. Since gold's value remains constant, its price fluctuations, therefore, reflect the dollar's volatility. This needs to be hammered home. It's not about gold. It's about the dollar.

**The Rap:** "There's not enough gold in the world to support the dollar at its present values." According to this reasoning, the United States has only about 261 million ounces of gold with a market price of roughly $500 billion. The monetary base is more than $6 trillion. Fixing the dollar to gold, this argument goes, would result in a savage deflation.

**Answer:** The gold standard is not about "supply" but about maintaining stable currency value. You don't need to have piles of this precious metal for a gold standard to work. Gold simply serves as the anchor of value. A gold standard functions much like the commodity standard used by Volcker and Greenspan. The gold price is the barometer that enables you to maintain a stable dollar value. Price of gold getting too high or too low? You adjust the money supply appropriately. Even during the heyday of the classical gold standard, no country ever had 100 percent gold backing for its money. Great Britain often had very low amounts of gold backing the pound. The quantity in other countries varied widely, too. If the United States decided to have convertibility—to give people the legal right to redeem dollars for gold at a fixed rate and *vice versa*—the US government still has enough of the metal to make such a system work, even with the Fed's bloated balance sheet.

**The Rap:** "A gold standard means that the government would not be able to expand the money supply."

**Answer:** Wrong. The money supply can grow as much as is needed to support a growing economy, while maintaining a stable currency value. We've previously noted that, from 1775 to 1900, the money supply in the United States mushroomed 160-fold even though the dollar was fixed to gold. Between 1934 and 1971, the US dollar monetary base became ten times larger, while the dollar was fixed to gold at the rate of $35 an ounce. This supported the economic growth of the late 1940s, 1950s, and 1960s.

**The Rap:** "The gold standard caused the Great Depression."

**Answer:** The answer is, "No, it didn't." Contrary to what is often alleged, even gold's most outspoken critics don't blame gold for the Depression. The most pointed charge leveled against gold, by prominent monetary historian Barry Eichengreen, was that the gold standard didn't exactly cause the Great Depression, but amplified its effects.

John Maynard Keynes also did not blame the gold standard for the Great Depression, nor did many of his successors. Their actual objection was that gold blocked the inflationism—the currency devaluation and interest rate manipulation—that they believed would boost the economy and end the downturn.

The real cause of the beginning of the Great Depression was the Smoot-Hawley Tariff Act. This shocking and totally unprecedented legislation ended up imposing an average 60 percent tax on *more than 3,000* import items. It was the equivalent of exploding a bomb that devastated the global trading system.

The enactment of Smoot-Hawley set off a worldwide trade war as disruptive to global commerce as the start of World War I in 1914. The economy crashed, and so did tax revenues.

Governments around the globe didn't know what hit them. Their response to this initial recession was a blizzard of tax increases—in other words, austerity—that only deepened the downturn. The worst offenders were Germany, Britain, and the US. In 1932, the US enacted a huge tax increase; the top income tax rate, for example, jumped from 25 percent to 63 percent, deepening the slump. By 1936, it had reached 79 percent.

**The Rap:** "The gold standard stood in the way of Britain's recovery from the Depression." According to this argument, Britain's economy rallied when the country went off the gold standard and floated the pound in late 1931.

**Answer:** The move produced a temporary boost. But Britain soon had to raise interest rates to prop up its plunging pound. Moreover, the devaluation led to a collapse in the value of British pound-denominated bonds held throughout Europe and the world. Investors in what was considered the risk-free asset of the time were thrown into financial peril. Other countries followed with their own devaluations. At least twenty countries weakened their currencies. The United States devalued in 1933. Belgium followed in 1935. Italy and France did the same in 1936, as did Switzerland. These "beggar-thy-neighbor" devaluations prolonged the Depression.

Today's Keynesian academics may cheer devaluations, but not the people who have actually lived through them. The trauma of the 1930s led the world's nations to seek an end to the instability of fiat currencies. In 1944, allies and neutral nations convened in New Hampshire and created a new international monetary system, the Bretton Woods gold standard.

## CHAPTER FIVE

# What About Your Money?

W HAT DOES all of this mean for your money? Can you preserve and even grow your assets so that you stay ahead of inflation?

There's no simple formula. During the stagflation of the 1970s, *Forbes* magazine featured on its cover a block of ice in the desert sheltered by an umbrella. The title read: "Inflation: How to Protect Your Capital." The magazine warned readers: "We cannot tell a lie. Given our tax laws and today's virulent rate of inflation, there is no reliable way for the individual investor to hang on to his capital, let alone expand it by investing. Hold on to your pocketbook if anyone tells you otherwise."

Inflation has been at the top of the news since the pandemic. How bad are things going to get? The answer you'll hear will depend on the pundit and the cable channel. It's often said, for example, that stock market returns over time outpace inflation. That's true. But what about the short term?

The answer is that things can get rocky. A serious inflation, like the kind the US experienced during the 1970s, can mean more roller-coaster volatility—stomach-turning market dives, combined with dizzying stock price run-ups. At the same time, those supposed market highs may not be what they seem. They may reflect the price distortions of inflation and not real increases in value. During the 1970s, the inflation-adjusted Dow Jones Industrial Average fell more than 50 percent. In the first decade of the twenty-first century, the inflation-adjusted Dow experienced a decline of similar magnitude.

In this environment, it may not be possible to "hedge against inflation." But it does help to be an informed investor. The purpose of this chapter is to provide some tools to help you sort through the flood of often contradictory information and make better investment decisions.

## Figuring Out What's Going On

Diagnosing a financial malaise is a little like diagnosing a medical illness. You look at the symptoms reflected by a variety of indicators and reach a conclusion.

**The Consumer Price Index (CPI).** One such indicator is the Consumer Price Index prepared by the Bureau of Labor Statistics (https://www.bls.gov/cpi/). The index measures prices paid by urban consumers for a basket of consumer goods and services. Along with the US "CPI," there are indexes for specific geographic areas. The CPI's website contains comparative price data for specific product categories like automotive fuel and food. You can find monthly releases with monthly "year-over-year" average price increases for all items, and for specific product categories.

Critics, however, point out that the CPI has weaknesses. The methodology—that is, the basket of goods whose prices are measured by the index—has changed over the years. The CPI also doesn't include price data for major expenditures like health insurance, which is largely paid for by employers, or government programs like Medicare or Medicaid.

Also, the CPI may be underestimating inflation because it ignores changes in consumer behavior in response to higher prices. For example, families may be spending the same amount on meat. But now they're buying cheaper cuts. There are different versions of the CPI and other indexes that attempt to adjust for these shortcomings.

**The CPI Inflation Calculator.** An offshoot of the index, the CPI Inflation Calculator can tell you how much the dollar's purchasing power has dropped over a stretch of time. (No, it almost never increases.) According to the calculator, $1.00 in the year 2000 had the same buying power as $1.62 by 2021. If you do the math, you'll find out that the greenback's buying power has declined by 38 percent.

**The Personal Consumption Expenditures Price Index (PCE).** Favored by Fed economists, the PCE is an index of prices much like the CPI, only based on a different formula. It captures inflation, or deflation, across a wide range of consumer expenses. Unlike the CPI, it includes the cost of health-care services paid for by third-party insurance.

However, all price indexes are flawed indicators because

they focus on prices which, as we've pointed out, are only symptoms of inflation and not the "illness." The depreciation of currency can take time to show up in the cost of living. Thus, the government's numbers likely understate the level of inflation. For example, the annual inflation level in July 2020, according to the CPI, was around 1 percent. But people were already feeling the rise in prices and no one trusted those numbers. Sadly, they were right. Less than one year later, the CPI showed 5 percent inflation.

## The Best Inflation Indicators

If you want to know what's happening to the value of the dollar, gold is where you should look first. Plenty of websites carry up-to-the-minute spot gold prices.

**How to Read the Gold Price.** When the price of gold rises— in other words, when more money is needed to buy an ounce of gold—that usually means the dollar's value has *decreased*. A brief spike in the gold price, however, does not necessarily signal inflation. Daily price movements may not be significant. But, if the price goes up and stays there for an extended period, or if it fluctuates but the general trend is up, that signals a downturn in the value of the dollar.

**Commodity Prices.** You should also look at other commodity prices. Commodities like oil, silver, and wheat are more sensitive to supply and demand changes than gold. Their prices may rise and fall due to reasons unrelated to currency values. But, like gold, their prices will rise if the dollar declines. Commodity prices, however, typically lag gold. So, a rise in the gold price—and a decline in dollar value—might not be reflected in higher commodity prices until twelve months later.

Of the commodities other than gold, oil is usually the best indicator of the dollar's direction. *Usually,* though not always. The soaring oil prices of the early 1970s were a direct reaction to the dollar's devaluation after the Nixon Shock. But oil can also reflect genuine fluctuations in supply and demand. In 2021, rising oil prices were due not only to a weaker dollar but also to increasing demand for oil as the economy reopened, and the Biden administration's new restrictions on domestic energy production.

The prices of individual commodities can be found on business news sites such as the *Wall Street Journal*, Fox Business, Bloomberg, and CNBC, where they're tracked minute-to-minute. Also check commodity indexes like the Commodity Research Bureau Index (CRB), the Bloomberg Commodity Spot Index, and the Standard & Poor's/Goldman Sachs Commodity Index (S&P GSCI).

**What Is the Fed Doing?** In addition to checking the price of gold and commodities, it helps to know the direction of the Federal Reserve's monetary policy. What is the central bank's target for the Federal Funds rate? That's the interest rate influencing how much financial institutions can charge borrowers, and the amount of money that flows into the economy. A low Federal Funds rate, therefore, can be a sign that the Fed is creating too much money. You should also look at whether or not the Fed is paying interest on the money banks have parked at the Fed (i.e., their reserves). If the central bank is raising the rate they pay on reserves, that may signal concern about inflation.

The central bank's bond purchases or sales are also an important indication of where the value of the dollar is headed. Is the Fed continuing its bond purchases and further expanding the money supply? Or, is it shrinking the monetary base by selling those securities? The answers may be found on the Federal Reserve balance sheet.

**Reading the Fed's Balance Sheet.** The central bank's assets and liabilities are published on the central bank's "statistical release" (also known as document H.4.1). The Fed issues these numbers every Thursday on www.federalreserve.gov. Document H.4.1 summarizes the total amount of currency in circulation, as well as what the Fed holds in securities, gold, foreign currencies, and other assets.

The release also contains information about those reverse repos that the Fed has been using to mask its expansion of the money supply. Scroll down to "Factors Affecting Reserve Balances of Depository Institutions," and look at the data on "reverse repurchase agreements."

**Where to Get Money Supply Information.** Another release on the Fed's website called "Money Stock Measures" (H.6) provides more details about the state of the money supply. It tells you, for instance, how much money is in circulation and how much is in bank reserves.

**A Quick Guide to "the M's."** The various measures of the supply of money are known as "the M's." The key measures are:

"M1" consisting of the most liquid forms of money: currency, traveler's checks, demand deposits, savings deposits, and other deposits against which checks can be written.

The next measure, "M2," includes M1 plus time deposits of less than $100,000, and balances in retail money-market mutual funds.

"M3" includes M2 plus large time deposits, institutional money market funds, short-term repurchase agreements (repos), and larger liquid assets.

Most important in terms of inflation is "M0," also known as the "monetary base" or "base money" consisting of currency in circulation plus bank cash reserves.

Another related indicator is the velocity of money, which tells you how actively money is used. In a hyperinflation, when people rush to get rid of increasingly worthless currency, velocity can skyrocket. It declines when there is less or even low inflation. You can find this indicator and other measures at the website for the St. Louis Federal Reserve.

**What About Government Debt?** When a government's finances get shaky, so does the value of its currency. Uncle Sam's federal debt burden is useful information when assessing the government's likely need to borrow and print money. What is the ratio of federal government debt to GDP? How much is the government borrowing in order to be able to pay interest on its bonds? The Treasury, the St. Louis Fed, and other sites have these statistics.

The final piece that completes the puzzle is what the government plans to spend. What is the media reporting? The dollar may fall if Washington looks like it will pass legislation with trillions of dollars in new spending that will likely be financed via more money creation. What's the current status of the debate? What statements are politicians putting out? What's the current state of the economy and the political environment? For example, when the economy slows, there is more pressure on the Fed to boost the economy by creating more dollars.

Congressional Budget Office projections found at www. cbo.gov can provide insights into the likely impact of new spending on government finances. These estimates, however, are based on controversial economic models.

Each of these numbers mean little in and of themselves. But taken together, they create a picture of where the value of the dollar is likely to go in the months ahead.

## SHOULD I REBALANCE MY PORTFOLIO?

What does this mean for your investments? We should all be thinking about this question, which has taken on new urgency in these increasingly perilous times.

The conventional wisdom has been that a "balanced" investment portfolio should be 60 percent stocks and 40 percent bonds. A 60/40 ratio is supposed to provide the best ratio between risk and return. Stocks provide growth at higher risk, while bonds provide steady, fixed income that's supposedly safe and low risk. Inflation turns this logic on its head.

With inflation eating away fixed incomes, any investment that pays a fixed return, such as a bond or a longer-term certificate of deposit, should be avoided. That doesn't mean you should make a headlong rush into stocks. Other investments that typically hold or appreciate in value include hard assets like real estate and precious metals including, most notably, gold.

Below are some guidelines that can help inform your decisions.

## STOCKS:
## APPRECIATION BUT NOT ALWAYS GROWTH

**Stocks.** Stocks have long been considered an "inflation hedge." Is that true? The answer is "yes—sort of." That's partly due to the fact that inflationary periods can start off with a buoyant economy. Larger players in certain industries benefit from government's newly created money. People spend their rising wages. Corporations rake in higher revenues. Devaluation lightens the burden of long-term debts. In this environment of "irrational exuberance," stock prices can appear to be rising with no end in sight. But very often, this is the Money Illusion.

Remember, prices are not real values. Look more closely at the numbers, and you'll discover a different picture. When inflation is taken into account, the economy, corporate growth—and the real value of stocks—may be slowing or actually declining.

When money stabilizes, stocks generally bounce back, but this takes place over a period of years. How can you minimize losses in the meantime?

**Physical Commodities and Commodities Futures.** The prices of commodities usually rise when currency values slide. That's why oil, wheat, and precious metals are generally considered a good place for money during times of inflation. However, with the exception of precious metals, it's not easy for the average person to directly buy commodities like oil. That is, unless you have your own storage facility and are prepared to take delivery.

Commodities futures are also highly speculative and not

for the inexperienced investor. Investing in futures is dangerous because you are effectively taking on debt, and you can easily get in over your head. Some Exchange Traded Funds have been developed which hold commodity futures. However, these have been somewhat problematic because of the short-term nature of futures contracts. For example, after ninety days, you might have to buy a new futures contract for, say, corn, possibly at a higher price. In other words, trading in futures is not like trading in shares of stock.

**Commodity-Based Equities.** People who wish to invest in commodities as an inflation hedge usually do so by buying shares of commodity producers. These stocks, however, won't give you the same appreciation as direct investments in the commodities themselves. For example, between 1969 and 1980, the price of oil went from $3 a barrel to almost $40 a barrel. During the same period, the stock price of oil giant Exxon roughly doubled. Exxon did far better than the stock market as a whole, but dramatically underperformed compared to oil or gold.

Another point to keep in mind is that much of the growth in these stocks usually occurs early. Price appreciation eventually slows as inflation pushes up expenses; in addition, managements that become flush with cash often start making bad capital-allocation decisions.

Case in point: in 1981, Exxon invested nearly $1 billion in a microprocessor producer called Zilog. The corporation was following the lead of oilfield services company Schlumberger, which had bought semiconductor manufacturer Fairchild in 1979. Neither investment performed well. A Zilog senior executive conceded years later that one reason for the company's failure to displace Intel was that Exxon gave them "too much money."

A surprising exception to the general rule regarding commodity-based stocks: gold mining companies. They have done rather poorly compared to gold in recent years. A better investment is gold mining *royalty* companies that provide financing to mining companies. Their share prices tend to do a better job of keeping pace with gold. In fact, they have outperformed bullion, and also the gold mining companies they finance, over the longer term. The largest company of this sort is Franco-Nevada Corporation (FNV). Others active in this sector include Royal Gold (RGLD), Sandstorm Gold (SAND), and Osisko Gold Royalties (OR).

**Commodity-Based Exchange Traded Funds.** If you prefer to spread the risk, another alternative is Exchange Traded Funds (ETFs) that enable you to invest in a basket of companies in a particular industry. There are energy ETFs that include a collection of oil and gas producers. Other ETFs focus on mining and agriculture.

**Look for Stocks with High Profit Margins.** Inflation means you need to think a little differently when selecting individual stocks. Warren Buffett has pointed out that "earnings reported in corporate financial statements are no longer the dominant variable that determines whether there are any real earnings for you, the owner." A company may have strong earnings. But does it have sufficient cash flow to replace inventories or equipment whose prices have skyrocketed? Companies with smaller margins are more likely to get in trouble when production costs go up. During inflationary times, the numbers may not fully reflect corporations' real profit and loss.

Individual investors need to consider how well a company is equipped to weather inflation's rising costs. Coca-Cola, for instance, did relatively well during the seventies because its product was basically sugar and water and some flavor. The strength of the Coca-Cola brand enabled the company to sell this at a high margin.

**How Much "Pricing Power?"** Other questions to keep in mind include: How easy is it for a company to raise prices and pass higher costs on to consumers? Are prices regulated? How likely are people to want to pay more for their product? Companies with strong brands that can raise prices without a drop in demand for their products have "pricing power" that can help them better cope with inflation.

Consider manufacturers of consumer items people depend on. Producers of food or household paper goods, for instance, can raise prices more easily. But a company that relies on borrowing to expand may run into problems. Generally, it's a good idea to avoid companies with huge cash needs such as utilities that need to spend on modernizing plants and equipment, and whose prices are regulated.

**High-Dividend Stocks.** Stocks paying healthy dividends can be a good substitute for bonds that no longer pay a decent return. Standard & Poor's issues an annual list of "Dividend Aristocrats," S&P stocks that have increased their dividend payment for at least the past twenty-five consecutive years. They include stocks like ExxonMobil, which pays a stratospheric 5.71 percent dividend, Clorox, which pays 2.41 percent, and Proctor & Gamble, which pays 2.57 percent. These aren't exciting growth stocks. But steady income can make up for the lack of glamour. It's also comforting to know that they've been around long enough to have weathered past crises.

**Think Short- and Long-Term.** Make a distinction between your retirement money, where you invest for the longer term, and your non-retirement portfolio where you may take a little more risk. Continue to contribute regularly to your retirement account. This will benefit from what's called *dollar cost averaging.* For example, invest a fixed dollar amount each month in a broad, low-cost index fund. Don't stop if there's a downturn. Console yourself with the knowledge that you're getting more shares for your money. Inevitably the market rebounds, usually when you least expect it. Your bonus: your gain is bigger.

For retirement portfolios, we recommend sticking with index funds that cover a broad range of stocks such as the S&P 500. It is best to stay away from specialized index funds, which need more active management.

**Cash? Yes, Cash.** This may sound counterintuitive. You may worry: Won't the value of my money get eaten away? What if your portfolio gets socked by the kind of savage market slide we saw during the financial crisis of 2008? That's precisely why it's good to keep a cash reserve along with your stocks even during inflationary times. There may be some loss of value. But better to have cash on hand for an emergency than to have to sell a stock at a loss.

Cash may not seem like a good place to park money in

this period of zero-percent interest rates. But eventually interest rates will rise. Remember, rising interest rates are common during inflationary periods. This is very bad for stocks and bonds. But during the inflationary 1970s, owners of cash earned more interest as rates rose. Inflationary conditions can be quite bad for stocks, which can fall to low valuations. Having cash allows you to buy stocks when they are cheap.

**Your Non-Retirement Portfolio.** This is where you can afford to take more risk. Your non-retirement account is where you might keep your commodities stocks, and stocks of growth companies that you've decided can weather inflation, like Amazon and Google.

Don't worry. Equities will take hits, but they always come back. The market has averaged annual returns of more than 9 percent for more than a century. The market lost more than 50 percent of its value in the crash of 2007–2009. But, by 2014, stocks were not only back, they had about tripled from their lows. Inflation can be a bad time for stocks. But it can be a great time to buy stocks cheaply.

**SPACs.** An investment vehicle that has become enormously popular is "special purpose acquisition companies," better known as SPACs. A SPAC is a speculative device that enables a company to, in effect, go public without a formal Initial Public Offering. SPACs raise money to buy what they think are promising companies. But you're investing before the SPAC buys anything. In other words, you're investing on the promise that managers of a SPAC will find a good investment. Meanwhile, those managers can get juicy fees even if the investment doesn't work out. Our advice: proceed with caution. Do your homework.

## BONDS:
## NOT WHAT THEY USED TO BE

In the high-interest-rate period of the late 1970s, bonds issued by states, local government authorities, and municipalities were a popular way of obtaining a steady, tax-free income in the face of inflation. That has changed in this era of artificially low interest rates.

Say you buy a 30-year Treasury bond that pays 2.4 percent interest. What happens if the Fed finally decides to raise rates and long-term rates go to 4.8 percent? The price of the bond goes down because the interest rate is locked in. You've lost about half of its value. Even short-term bonds don't provide enough return in a zero-interest-rate environment.

**Some Tips About TIPS.** In the late 1990s, the federal government tried to mitigate this effect by creating Treasury Inflation-Protected Securities (TIPS) as a way around inflation. The bond's principal—i.e., its value when bought or sold—is readjusted for inflation every six months. For example, you buy a 10-year TIPS bond for $1,000 with an interest rate of 1 percent. During that time, inflation averages 7 percent. When the bond matures, you would get $2,000 of principal instead of the $1,000. The interest rates on TIPS bonds are fixed. As the bond's principal is adjusted for inflation, interest payments to you rise accordingly.

TIPS are often recommended as an inflation hedge. But

the price for TIPS bonds now is very high. Therefore, you would need considerable inflation to make them worthwhile.

## Real Estate:
## Words of Warning

Real estate is a popular "hard asset" investment during inflationary periods. Typical families have more money in their home than in stocks, bonds, or gold. A house offers the benefit of price appreciation when currency values decline, and also a place to live. But there are disadvantages.

During the 1970s, US housing prices rose 148 percent—far less than gold or oil but nonetheless a substantial gain. During the Great Inflation, people who bought their suburban house for $40,000 in 1968 discovered a decade later that that house was now worth $150,000. They had borrowed just $30,000 and now they had all this equity. It was a giant slam dunk for a lot of suburbanites during that period.

Another advantage of housing as an inflation investment is that fixed, long-mortgage obligations are lightened over time as currency values fall. Wages that have risen due to inflation can make those fixed mortgage payments look tiny. The three biggest homebuilding booms of the last seventy years came during inflationary periods after the US went off the gold standard: in 1973, 1979, and during the housing bubble of the early 2000s.

**A "Surefire" Investment That Can Backfire.** Despite all of that, you must weigh some very real risks. Don't buy more house than you can pay for at today's income and prices. Remember those people who invested in housing in the early 2000s and later found themselves underwater after the Fed raised interest rates—and they were no longer able to shoulder their mortgages.

Another factor to consider is that a house can be very costly to maintain. Ask any homeowner who has had to foot the bill for extensive and often unexpected repairs, renovations, and maintenance. Obviously, a house is a very different asset than a stock. Think of it as an expensive consumer item that has the possibility of appreciation, but not a guarantee of one.

**A Good "Refi" Opportunity.** Today's low-interest-rate environment, however, may be an opportunity to lower the interest rate of your existing mortgage. Try to get a fixed rate, since rates are more likely to go up, and not down, in the future. Be sure your agreement allows you to refinance later on.

What about buying a house to rent out? It's never easy to be a landlord. But if you're bent on buying a rental property as a business, make sure you can pass along rent increases that may be necessary as the cost of living goes up. Unfortunately, rent controls are common during periods of monetary inflation. The effect on property can be catastrophic. During the inflation nightmare of the 1970s, it was widely suspected that desperate New York City landlords unable to recoup expenses were actually burning down unprofitable buildings. The Bronx resembled a war zone.

**An Easier Way to Invest in Real Estate.** Consider buying shares of a Real Estate Investment Trust (REIT), a company that owns income-producing properties. By law, 90 percent of the profits from these properties have to be distributed to shareholders.

The drawback, however, is that REITs carry a high percentage of debt, which makes them a potentially volatile investment if property values or rental incomes fall. But this can also be an advantage if inflation reduces debt burdens. REITs were highly attractive in 2000, when their yields were near 8 percent. Unfortunately, much has changed since then. More recently, yields on REITs have hovered between 2 and 3 percent, on average.

It's possible to buy shares of Exchange Traded Funds consisting of REITs. Popular diversified REIT ETFs include the Vanguard Real Estate ETF (VNQ) and the iShares Global REIT ETF (REET).

There are different kinds of REITs. Timber REITs represent income from harvesting timber. This amounts to a type of agricultural commodity, which also has a connection with homebuilding and construction. The three largest timberland REITs are Weyerhaeuser (WY), Rayonier (RYN) and Potlatch Deltic Corporation (PCH).

A few REITs have emerged that lease farmland. The returns on farmland leasing tend to mirror the prices of agricultural commodities over the long term. This category may expand in the future, and represents an interesting way to get exposure to agricultural commodities. US farmland REITs include Gladstone Land (LAND) and Farmland Partners (FPI).

**What About Commercial Real Estate?** Office buildings, warehouses, and shopping malls are another investment category. Here again, it's crucial to do detailed investigation. Traditionally, as we have noted, hard assets are good inflation hedges. But not all hard assets are the same. For example, there appears to be a serious glut of commercial office space in cities like New York and San Francisco. Many malls, meanwhile, have been hurt by the growth of online shopping. By contrast, the booming online market has boosted warehouses, needed by companies like Amazon and Walmart.

## Gold and Other Precious Metals

The idea of owning gold may conjure up images of King Midas atop his throne beside a chest of gold coins. Gold is more of a hedge against inflation than an investment. That's why gold should make up no more than 10 percent of your portfolio. Its price may rise, but it does not appreciate in real worth like an investment in Amazon or Apple.

Normally, there is nothing especially exciting about investing in gold bullion. Gold pays no dividends and has no cashflow. Gold's primary characteristic and greatest advantage is that it is stable. However, during periods when the dollar is losing value, the price of gold rises—a lot.

Having a small percentage of your money in gold is a hedge against a weakening dollar. For example, during the inflationary period that began in the late 1960s, gold was priced at $35 an ounce. Recently, it was priced around $1,800 an ounce. This is evidence that the value of the dollar has fallen by about 98 percent since then. In other words, while the worth of the dollar declines, gold maintains its value unchanged.

**How to Buy Gold.** Online retail dealers like APMEX (apmex.com) or SD Bullion (sdbullion.com) offer to both buy and sell coins and bars. If you do buy gold, you need to keep an eye on it, as you would any investment. At the end of an inflationary period, when currency values are stabilized—even if the CPI is still rising—gold will disappoint. The yellow metal crashed to less than $300 an ounce in the summer of 1982 from a high of more than $800 an ounce when the Fed was killing inflation. For the next two decades, the gold price usually fluctuated between $350–$400 an ounce. At some point it may make sense to sell your gold and buy something else. When inflationary periods come to an end, other assets, like stocks, can be cheap.

You can think of gold as a particularly reliable kind of cash, which is the role it has, in fact, played for centuries. There may be an opportunity to use this cash to buy productive assets at very good prices.

**Silver.** At one time, silver maintained a fairly stable value in relation to gold. Since the late 1800s, when an ounce of gold was roughly worth sixteen ounces of silver, this longstanding relationship has broken down. While gold is still a sort of cash, silver has become an industrial metal and a speculative vehicle. Today, it takes more than seventy ounces of silver to buy one ounce of gold. Nevertheless, it can be an inflation hedge in certain circumstances. For instance, it is best to buy silver when its value versus gold falls to historical lows, as it did in 2020. Silver still retains some vague monetary characteristics. Unlike most commodities, you can easily own it directly and store it in a vault. It won't rot or rust. However, if gold is steadfast and predictable, silver has become wild and woolly.

**Precious Metals ETFs.** Both gold and silver can be purchased via ETFs which hold metal in vaults. Unfortunately, there is some controversy as to whether some of the most popular ETFs actually hold all the metal that they imply. You should research which ETFs are currently considered the most trustworthy and reliable.

FORBES, LEWIS & AMES

**Other Tangible Assets.** An often-touted place to park money during inflation is in so-called "alternative investments." They include tangible assets such as fine art, stamps, antiques, and other collectibles. A new entry into this category is the "NFT" or *non-fungible token.* This blockchain-based digital asset grants the owner rights to a specific property, such as art or real estate. NFTs launched by celebrities like Grimes have become the rage.

The problem with such alternatives, however, is that they are risky places to park your money. Art and antique values can depend on fickle popular tastes. Always keep in mind that these items are not always easy to turn into cash. Not to mention that prices can reflect an inflation-fueled mania to "buy anything." Some NFTs, for example, have gone for astronomical prices.

## WHAT ABOUT CRYPTOS?

Cryptocurrencies like Bitcoin, Ethereum, Dogecoin, and others have been gaining ground as alternatives to traditional money. Their vocal supporters include tech visionaries like Elon Musk. Companies like Musk's Tesla, and also PayPal, have experimented with accepting cryptos as payment. Crypto fans are watching to see how well El Salvador does with its experiment of making Bitcoin legal tender. But, so far, most people aren't using them for everyday commercial purposes. That's because, while cryptos may function in some applications as a payment system, the overwhelming majority of them are not reliable money. At least, not yet.

Money, we have explained throughout this book, is fundamentally a measuring tool, like a clock that measures time or a scale that measures weight. To be able to function like those other instruments, cryptos must be seen as having a stable value. Right now, most don't. Cryptos may have been invented as an alternative to unsound money. But at the moment they're even more volatile. Bitcoin has been known to lose half its value in a single day.

It is true that a number of people who have invested in roller-coaster digital currencies have done well. But in a non-inflationary environment, cryptos could well plummet the way oil did when inflation was conquered in the early 1980s. Cryptos are an innovation with enormous potential. But until they become genuinely sound money, they're primarily just a speculative football. They might go up, or they might go down because that's what speculative footballs do. But they don't provide a real alternative to stocks, bonds, or both.

A new class of cryptocurrencies has recently appeared called "stablecoins." They're tied to a specific item, such as the dollar, gold, or a basket of commodities. The investment potential of these cryptos reflects the asset they're tied to and is usually fairly limited. One of the best known stablecoins is Tether. Compared with Bitcoin, it offers the advantage of a link to the relatively stable dollar. The digital currency's comparative stability is likely why its circulation in 2021 more than tripled.

Along with this success, however, has come growing concerns that these cryptos may not always live up to their billing. Tether, for instance, has been criticized for not being backed with a sufficient reserve of dollars. This problem must be addressed. Tether and other stablecoins should be guaranteed by assets that are in the custody of a reputable third party and easily verifiable. In other words, there has to be transparency. If stablecoins can be trusted to be truly stable more people will start using them, and they may begin to compete with fiat currencies like the dollar to become an inflation hedge like gold.

## WHAT TO DO WHEN INFLATION ENDS

Yes, inflation *will* end. In the 1970s, people thought that price increases would continue forever, until Paul Volcker finally stabilized the dollar. Eventually, currencies stop declining in value.

How will you know when this is happening? If the price of gold falls or remains steady for a while, that can mean that the dollar is starting to stabilize. But the critical question is: Will this stability be lasting or temporary? That depends on the political environment. Have policymakers finally awakened to the need for a stable dollar? A period of stability can be followed by another round of currency decline, as we experienced in the early 2000s.

If things appear to be moving in the right direction and money is stabilizing, you will need to rethink your portfolio. Commodity-related investments you made when the dollar fell may stop rising, or even crash.

When Paul Volcker ended the Great Inflation, the result was a wrenching deflation that saw the price of oil collapse from $37 a barrel in 1980 to eventually around $14 a barrel in 1986. After Ronald Reagan was elected president in 1980, the price of gold was about $650 an ounce. Volcker's actions knocked the yellow metal to a low of $300 an ounce. Anyone who'd hung on to investments in oil or gold during those years suffered serious losses.

The end of inflation is the time to sell your commodity investments. Gold mining equities may have reached extremely high valuations and should be sold. Other commodity producers may begin a period of very bad performance, as overinvestment leads to a glut. It also makes sense to sell your gold and acquire bonds or cash, whose value has stabilized or may even increase.

At the same time, the end of inflation presents new opportunities. Even after a currency stops falling, prices may continue to rise for several years afterwards. However, the price increases of this "inflationary tailwind" may not fully convey the very real increases in *value* resulting from the newly-stabilized currency. This is, in effect, the Money Illusion in reverse. In this situation, you can realize some real growth in bonds, as well as stocks.

**Look at Financial Stocks.** When a country emerges from severe inflation, banks are often among the best-performing companies. That's because people generally like to minimize holding cash when it is being devalued. But as the economy recovers, interest rates can be very high; people and companies low on cash can have a desperate need to borrow. Bank returns on equity can hit triple digits. This was common in Eastern Europe following the hyperinflation of the 1990s.

Investors should also be aware that the emergence from inflation can present new challenges for businesses. We explained earlier that inflation is a boon to debtors. Newly sound money, however, means that debts are no longer being inflated away. If there are lingering high interest rates, they may become more difficult to pay. Just as bankruptcies decline during periods of inflation, when inflation ends there can be a surge in bankruptcies as corporations attempt to restructure debt.

For example, in the US during the 1980s the economy

boomed when inflation was ended. Nonetheless, sectors like agriculture and energy went through wrenching contractions before they recovered.

## INFLATION'S SILVER LINING FOR THE ECONOMY

The good news is that, in the past, the end of inflation has meant a return to pro-market policies. The process of stabilizing a currency usually involves enacting economy-friendly reforms, such as lower taxes and a less-burdensome regulatory environment. That happened in Japan and Germany in the early 1950s, when people like Ludwig Erhard, Ikeda Hayato, and Joseph Dodge brought lower taxes and stable money reforms that ended both nations' post-war hyperinflation. Between 1950 and 1970, Japan's GDP, as measured in dollars, grew sixteen times larger, with an average nominal GDP growth rate of 14.9 percent per year.

In the US and Britain, the Great Inflation of the 1970s and early 1980s was followed by the tax and regulatory reforms of Ronald Reagan and Margaret Thatcher. Many leaders of countries worldwide followed their example. Even the Soviet Union started to make free-market changes in its economy, but such moves were too small and ineffectual to prevent the country from falling apart into fifteen nations in 1991.

Hyperinflationary disasters in Eastern Europe during the 1990s led to a period of currency reliability. "Flat tax" income-tax systems adopted by more than a score of governments worldwide also resulted in incredible economic performance. Nominal GDP growth rates of flat tax-adopting countries reached more than 20 percent per annum, with a currency of stable value. These post-inflation reforms led to amazing bull markets.

*The "$1 trillion coin" proposed by some advocates of Modern Monetary Theory.*

## CHAPTER SIX

# The Way Forward

A T THE BEGINNING of this book, we told the story of Zimbabwe's $100 trillion note that is a symbol of over-the-top hyperinflation. The "Zimbabwe dollar" has long been regarded with amusement. After all, who could imagine anything so crazy in this country? Well, think again.

The need for dollars to fill Uncle Sam's ever-widening maw of federal debt has become so great that, in 2021, some economists have pushed the idea of minting a $1 trillion coin to be deposited at the Federal Reserve to help the government pay its bills.

The proposal for the $1 trillion coin was shot down, even ridiculed. Nobody's asking "Are we Zimbabwe?" Nonetheless, there are very real clouds on the horizon concerning prospects for future inflation. They include current Washington policies that are slowing recovery from the pandemic. Taxes, regulations, and unnecessary spending are placing roadblocks in the way of growth and saddling Uncle Sam with an ever-increasing need to borrow and to print money. Recently inflamed relations with China and Russia, as well as tensions in the Middle East, also raise the possibility of new conflicts that may impact the global economy and the financial system.

In late 2021, Fed chief Jerome Powell announced that he would slightly hasten "tapering"—i.e., reducing the Fed's bond buying/money creation—to address the unexpectedly intense inflation. However, given the Fed's excesses of recent years, this may be too little too late. And who knows where the pandemic and its various variants will take our domestic politics? The far-left is putting pressure on the Fed to adhere to the socialist fantasy of Modern Monetary Theory, and expand its mandate to address issues like "climate change." Such efforts are causing the central bank to stray ever further from its original mission of protecting the dollar's integrity.

None of these developments bode especially well for an end to inflation. Then there are those barriers that have been artificially holding back the inflationary tide. We noted earlier that international banking regulations increased the amount of money banks had to hold on reserve. This prevented the Fed's spectacular money creation of the past several years from overwhelming the economy. And what about those reverse repos—the constant borrowing and repaying of bank loans? They have also helped keep the money supply from ballooning—at least on paper. Sooner or later, observers fear, these barriers may well break, resulting in an inflationary deluge.

Yet, there are some good reasons why a replay of the 1970s is not inevitable. In fact, it is very possible that recent events may prove to be a turning point—an opportunity to open the discussion about ending inflation by returning to stable money and a gold standard.

For one thing, the twenty-first century is not the 1970s, when there was no Internet or cable television to do a deep dive into a subject and endlessly discuss and debate. Back then, people didn't get constant breaking news notifications on their handhelds. They didn't live with a big news story 24/7. Today, inflation, for the first time in decades, is that story. Americans are getting constant updates about spikes in gas and food prices, and record increases in the CPI. They're able to process this information in a way they couldn't forty years ago. Individuals who might not have previously paid attention are hearing warnings about the connection between today's dangerous level of government spending and the rising prices that have been eating away at their paychecks. Younger people struggling to pay off student loans are learning that their salaries are being inflated away so that Uncle Sam can keep printing and borrowing zero-interest-rate free money, and they don't like what they're hearing.

Something else is happening, too. The rise of social media and the recent pandemic have raised doubts about the judgment of public officials, whose tweets and ever-changing declarations show them to be as human and fallible as the rest of us. In the words of *Newsweek*, the experience of COVID has "dealt an irreparable blow to the credibility of America's ruling class." That includes not only public-health bureaucrats but, presumably, central bankers. As the CPI continues to rise, more people will see through their opaque justifications for rising prices and conclude that they simply don't make sense.

Americans alarmed about the rise of socialism may also question a central banking system whose manipulation of money and interest rates comes perilously close to Soviet-style central planning. How can a handful of banking bureaucrats presume to make monetary policy that can effectively control the activity of a US economy comprised of 330 million people?

There are other reasons to be optimistic. One of them is the central truth that policymakers and Keynesians inevitably fail to grasp: governments may debase currency, but people instinctively seek monetary stability. Remember, that was why money was invented in the first place: to provide a trusted and unchanging unit of value. The need for stability is why, after the US abandoned gold, the euro was established by European nations seeking refuge from floating fiat currencies. It is why the Swiss franc is in high demand on the global markets. It is also why the Bank of England and the young United States, centuries earlier, ended inflation by pegging their money to gold, which set off an explosion of prosperity that changed the world.

So how do we recover monetary sanity and return to a healthy economy with low inflation? The first step is for citizens to promote awareness of the principles of sound money. The following takeaways from this book can help.

**1. Money loses value and you get inflation when the dollar is no longer trusted as a reliable unit of worth.** We discard a clock when it breaks down and no longer can be trusted to tell time. Or throw away a scale that stops working. The same applies to money. People lose faith in a currency that is no longer reliable, or whose supply is increasing beyond all reasonable need. Demand decreases. Money loses value. You get inflation.

## 2. A rise in the gold price means the dollar has lost value.

The yellow metal is the most stable commodity in the world. Therefore, when the price of gold rises, that means that more dollars are needed to buy gold. In other words, the dollar's value has declined. Gold's stable value is what makes it the best barometer of the worth of the dollar, or any other currency. Skeptics commonly claim that we can't go back to a gold monetary standard because gold is "unstable." Nothing is farther from the truth. If the dollar was stable, the price of gold wouldn't fluctuate.

## 3. There are two types of inflation. One is a response to market conditions and is usually temporary. The other, which results when governments or central banks corrupt currency, is far more dangerous.

Non-monetary inflation resulting from government mismanagement—such as the pandemic supply chain disruptions—is painful. But the effects are usually limited to specific sectors of the economy. Prices relax, for instance, when the supply chain problems are resolved. But with monetary inflation, which results when governments and central banks destroy a currency, the damage is far more widespread. This second type of inflation corrodes wealth, distorts markets, and debases social behavior. This is as true of a 2 percent rate of inflation as it is of higher levels of inflation. You might say monetary inflation is a "human-caused" disaster, responsible for centuries of economic and social destruction, from the fall of Rome to the 2006 implosion of the subprime mortgage market. Unfortunately, many people, including economists, will confuse the two types of inflation because of the Money Illusion—the natural tendency to see our own currency as stable. Rising prices are thought to signal changes in real world supply and demand, when they are actually distortions caused by too much Fed-created "easy money." This misperception is why monetary inflation, even at low levels, will lead to unnatural activity and artificially overheated markets, the so-called "bubbles" that eventually collapse.

**4. Higher prices are the *effect*, and not the cause, of monetary inflation.** Remember your imaginary vacation in Mexico. Those souvenirs whose prices shot up since your last visit did not suddenly become more valuable. The reason is that you now get twenty pesos to the dollar, compared with three pesos to the dollar thirty years ago. The culprit is the shrinking peso. In much the same way, we can tell that the dollar has lost value by comparing it to gold, whose intrinsic value doesn't change. Most so-called solutions to inflation fail because they make the mistake of artificially trying to control prices, instead of addressing the real cause, which is the loss of currency value.

**5. No nation, including the US, can inflate its way to prosperity.** There's no getting around it. Central bank policies that intentionally create "a little inflation" do not create wealth. There may be a burst of activity, but this is artificial and eventually subsides. Inflation-distorted prices destroy savings and corrupt markets. Investment is misdirected away from growth- and job-creating ventures into wealth-preservation and tax avoidance. The economy slows. The long-term result is fewer jobs and wealth destruction. If the US had the same growth rate today as it did in the 1950s and '60s, when the dollar was pegged to gold, per capita income would be

72 percent higher. Americans would be paid in dollars with more spending power. The economy would be at least 50 percent bigger.

**6. Moderate inflation results from short-term "stimulus;" hyperinflation comes from regular money printing to pay the government's bills.** The difference between moderate inflation and full-blown hyperinflation is more than a matter of magnitude. Moderate inflation is generally the result of a short-term event, such as a limited, Keynesian "stimulus" or the need to pay for a war. Hyperinflation occurs when governments regularly print money to finance the operation of government. This is illustrated by the Weimar Republic's hyperinflation. Sixty-three percent of the nation's total government spending in 1922 was financed by the printing press. Shutting down the printing press would have meant shutting down 63 percent of the government overnight. Present-day hyperinflaters like Venezuela and Argentina also routinely use money printing to pay their government's bills. In contrast, the fall in the value of the US dollar since 1970 has been due largely to the Fed's "easy money" response to conditions in the economy. The United States has not begun directly financing itself with large-scale money printing. Unfortunately, that may already be changing. Modern Monetary Theory, in favor with the current administration, contends that the Fed can simply print more money to fund government-welfare programs. This is the perfect formula for hyperinflation.

**7. Debasing money ultimately debases society.** Money was invented as a mutually agreed-upon unit of value that makes trade possible by facilitating trust between strangers. When people trade with sound and stable money, each side knows what they're getting from the exchange. But when money declines in value, this trust can be damaged or even destroyed. The devaluation of money inflates away savings and fixed incomes, while the rich and powerful can receive windfalls. In this way, inflation exacerbates inequality and fans the flames of grievance. Hence, the philosopher John Locke called inflation a "public failure of justice." The most severe inflationary episodes have been associated with social breakdown. Higher levels of crime, corruption, and social unrest can lead to political extremism and the rise of dictators. Currency devaluations have played a role in just about every major Great Disorder, from the fall of Rome to the inflation in Weimar Germany that set the stage for the rise of Adolf Hitler.

**8. Government spending is not about creating debt for your children. It's about creating inflation in the here and now.** We often hear well-intentioned warnings about ballooning government debt "being paid for by the next generation." The reality is that Americans start paying almost immediately through inflation's higher prices. Remember, inflation is a stealth tax that, as Keynes famously observed, allows government to confiscate the wealth of its citizens without being noticed. That is, until people realize their money no longer goes as far as it did.

**9. Sound money means "no inflation," but not "price stability."** Keynesians insist the Fed is needed to assure "price stability." That idea is a myth. There is no such thing as price stability, even during times of little or no inflation. Prices are the market's system of conveying information about supply and demand. They rise and fall all the time in a healthy economy. Higher prices, with their promise of higher profits, provide incentives to manufacturers to increase production. Eventually goods become more affordable. Cell phones that cost thousands of dollars when first introduced can now be bought for less than $50. During the gold-standard era of the 1800s, industrialization and higher productivity caused the cost of products from steel to kerosene to fall dramatically. At the same time, wages rose as Americans became more prosperous. By 1913, this kind of non-monetary wage "inflation" and goods "deflation" had made the United States the wealthiest country in the world. At no time were prices "stable," but the value of the dollar remained unchanged.

**10. The best way to end inflation, and to spur economic growth, is through a return to a sound dollar anchored by gold.** A gold standard simply links the greenback to gold, in much the same way that dozens of countries today link their currencies to the dollar or euro. The US relied on a sound dollar for nearly two centuries and it became the wealthiest country in the history of the world. Remember, money is, above all, a measure of worth. We should no more manipulate the dollar's value than we should float the number of inches in a ruler. And yet we have—with disastrous results.

The last fifty years of inflationary Fed policies and the floating fiat dollar has seen slower growth and more economic crises. According to one study, their frequency has doubled since the early 1970s, compared with the Bretton Woods and classical gold standard periods. That study was conducted *before* the financial meltdown of 2008.

With a gold standard, there would be no inflation. Full stop. A gold standard simply means that money has a fixed value and can fulfill its intended function as a trusted unit of worth.

Stable money and no inflation would mean more investment and a soaring economy. During the late 1800s era of the classical gold standard, when the US, England, most of Europe, and eventually Japan, linked their currencies to gold, more wealth was created during that century than all the previous centuries put together. The United States had what could be characterized as "full employment" (jobless rates of less than 5 percent) during most of the decade of the 1920s, and also the decade of the 1960s, when the dollar was pegged to gold.

Contrary to what many people believe, you don't necessarily need a large supply of gold to maintain a gold standard. A system could be phased in within about twelve months. After that, watch the economy take off!

Today Americans are decrying the emergence of "cancel culture," with its unprecedented suppression of unwanted ideas. Sadly, this one-sidedness is nothing new in official Washington, which has shut out any consideration of a return to the monetary principles that built America's storied prosperity, achieved through stable, gold-based money. The country is paying the penalty through rising prices and an ever-shrinking dollar.

It's high time to reopen the debate.

# Acknowledgments

OUR SPECIAL THANKS to Roger Kimball, prescient publisher of Encounter Books and *The New Criterion*, for seeing the possibilities of a book about inflation, long before the subject was at the top of the news. Thanks also to his superb team: production director Amanda DeMatto and manager Mary Spencer, who kept things on schedule; copy editor Justine Buchanan, who sharpened the final manuscript; marketing director Sam Schneider and director of publicity Lauren Miklos for raising awareness of the book; and Nola Tully and Rachel Williamson for providing essential legal and administrative support.

We are also grateful to the wonderful Elizabeth Daffin for her superlative research; Mikey Sabatella of ILMDesigns for designing the infographic; and Analiese Puzon and Delroy Tate for production services that went above and beyond.

Thanks also to others who helped in various ways: Mark

Skousen, Larry Reed, Heather Mac Donald, and Deroy Murdock.

This book owes a debt to Lewis Lehrman, Art Laffer, Larry Kudlow, Steve Hanke, Brian Domitrovic, Seth Lipsky, Amity Shlaes, Jim Grant, Ralph Benko, Steve Moore, John Fund, Judy Shelton, John Tamny, and George Gilder for work that has inspired us and done much to advance the understanding of economics and money.

Steve wants to express his appreciation to Forbes colleagues Merrill Vaughn, Jackie DeMaria, Emira Gjonbalaj, and Sue Radlauer, for crucial editorial and logistical assistance. He is also grateful to Bill Dal Col for his invaluable advice on so many occasions. And he is profoundly thankful for the support of his family, especially daughters Sabina, who provided research and practical help; Catherine, who has been indispensable for his being able to work so effectively despite the obstacles of COVID; and Moira, for insights on navigating various challenges.

Nathan would like to thank individuals and organizations that have supported his work, including: the Discovery Institute, James Turk, Sean Fieler and the American Principles Project, Forbes Media, the Cato Institute, the Heritage Foundation, Addison Wiggin and Agora Publishing, the American Institute for Economic Research, and the New York Society of Securities Analysts.

Finally, Elizabeth would like to express her appreciation to many of the people and institutions above, as well as to friends Laura and Gary Jacobs, Christine Creager, Clara Del Villar, Elizabeth and Jack Coleman, Betty Cammisa, and the Seltzer family, for their suggestions and encouragement.

# Endnotes

## INTRODUCTION

*ix* **"Inflation. The headlines are everywhere..."** Christopher Rugaber, "Why are Fears of Inflation Getting Worse?," Associated Press, May 12, 2021, https://apnews.com/article/financial-markets-inflation-health-coronavirus-pandemic-business-9b28c435b-caf8f787838ca1160e4d47f.

*ix* **"Consumer Prices Jump..."** Olivia Rockman, "U.S. Consumer Prices Jump Most Since 2008, Topping All Estimates," Bloomberg, July 13, 2121, https://www.bloomberg.com/news/articles/2021-07-13/u-s-consumer-prices-increased-in-june-by-more-than-forecast.

*ix* **"The front page of the *New York Post* proclaims..."** "The Incredible Shrinking Dollar," *New York Post*, July 14, 2021.

*ix* **"A shopper at a Long Island supermarket..."** Ben Popken, "Get Ready for Higher Grocery Bills for the Rest of the Year," NBC News, April 13, 2121, https://www.nbcnews.com/business/consumer/get-ready-higher-grocery-bills-rest-year-n1263897.

*ix* **"A Virginia car dealer..."** David Lynch, "Recovery's Stumbles Leave Americans Confronting Unfamiliar Inflation Risk," *Washington Post,* May 10, 2021.

*ix* **"A realtor in South Carolina..."** Chris Joseph, "Lumber Prices Skyrocketing, and Taking Home Prices with Them," WISTV, April 15, 2021, https://www.wistv.com/2021/04/15/lumber-prices-skyrocketing-taking-home-prices-with-them/.

*ix* **"Bloomberg News reports that customers..."** Justin Blum, "A $4,749 Bike Hints at Inflation Peril Looming for U.S. Economy," Bloomberg, June 5 2021, https://www.bloomberg.com/news/articles/2021-06-05/a-4-749-bike-hints-at-inflation-peril-looming-for-u-s-economy.

*x* **"Larry Summers, the Keynesian economist..."** Lawrence Lewitinn, "Lawrence Summers on Inflation: Fed 'Will Only Remove the Punch Bowl After It Sees People Staggering Around Drunk,'" CoinDesk, May 26, 2021, https://www.coindesk.com/markets/2021/05/26/lawrence-summers-on-inflation-fed-will-only-remove-the-punch-bowl-after-it-sees-people-staggering-around-drunk/.

*x* **"Summers went on to warn..."** Matt Egan, "Larry Summers Sends Stark Inflation Warning to Joe Biden," CNN Business, May 27, 2021, https://www.cnn.com/2021/05/26/economy/inflation-larry-summers-biden-fed/index.html.

*x* **"a decade of double-digit price increases..."** Alan Blinder, "The Anatomy of Double-Digit Inflation in the 1970s," *Inflation: Causes and Effects* (Chicago, University of Chicago Press, 1982), 261.

*xi* **"the price increases were 'transitory'..."** Patti Domm, "Inflation is Hotter Than Expected, But It Looks Temporary and Likely Won't Affect Fed Policy Yet," CNBC, June 10, 2121, https://www.cnbc.com/2021/06/10/inflation-hotter-than-expected-but-transitory-wont-affect-fed-policy.html.

*xi* **"Jerome Powell conceded..."** Mark DeCambre, "Powell Says Time to Retire 'Transitory' When Talking About Inflation—and Stock Markets Tank," MarketWatch.com, November 30, 2021, https://www.marketwatch.com/story/powell-says-time-to-retire-transitory-when-talking-about-inflationand-stock-markets-tank-11638305094.

*xi* **"breaks up the bottlenecks in our economy..."** Joseph Biden, "Remarks by President Biden on the Economy," transcript of address delivered in The White House Briefing Room, July 19, 2021, https://www.whitehouse.gov/briefing-room/speeches-remarks/2021/07/19/remarks-by-president-biden-on-the-economy-3/.

*xi* **"will enhance our productivity..."** Biden, "Remarks."

*xii* **"officials predicted a minimal level of only 1.8 percent inflation..."** Federal Reserve Open Market Committee, "Summary of Economic Projections," Federal Reserve, December 16, 2020, https://www.federalreserve.gov/monetarypolicy/fomcprojtabl20201216.htm.

*xii* **"PCE had shot past 5 percent..."** Bureau of Economic Analysis, "Personal Income and Outlays, October 2021," press release, November 24, 2021, https://www.bea.gov/news/2021/personal-income-and-outlays-october-2021.

*xii* **"*74 percent* of nominal GDP growth..."** "Inflation as Percent of Nominal GDP" (chart) *Unleash Prosperity Hotline*, Committee to Unleash Prosperity, #412, November 16, 2021 https://mailchi.mp/4ef82d29d331/unleash-prosperity-hotline-866180?e=f1a-6f760a8.

*xiii* **"the 'Nixon Shock,' imposed by President Richard Nixon..."** "Nixon and the End of the Bretton Woods System, 1971–1973," United States Department of State, https://history.state.gov/milestones/1969-1976/nixon-shock.

*xiii* **"has dropped by 98 percent..."** "Historical gold charts," Kitco, 2021, https://www.kitco.com/charts/historicalgold.html.

*xiv* **"Newton, with the help of his friend, the philosopher John Locke..."** Nathan Lewis, *Gold: The Monetary Polaris* (New Berlin, NY: Canyon Maple Publishing, 2013), 85.

Lewis, Nathan, *Gold: The Final Standard* (New Berlin, NY: Canyon Maple Publishing, 2019), 64-65.

Lewis, Nathan, *Gold: The Once and Future Money* (Hoboken, John Wiley & Sons, 2007), 29-30.

Forbes, Steve, and Elizabeth Ames, *MONEY: How the Destruction of the Dollar Threatens the Global Economy—and What We Can Do About It* (New York, McGraw Hill Education, 2014), 134.

*xiv* **"other European nations, as well as Japan..."** Forbes and Ames, *MONEY*, 135.

Lewis, Nathan, "The 1870-1914 Gold Standard: The Most Perfect One Ever Created," *Forbes*, January 3, 2013, https://www.forbes.com/sites/nathanlewis/2013/01/03/the-1870-1914-gold-standard-the-most-perfect-one-ever-created/?sh=362d63f34a6a.

Bordo, Michael David, *The Classical Gold Standard: Some Lessons for Today,* The Federal Reserve Bank of St. Louis, May 1981, 7, https://files.stlouisfed.org/files/htdocs/publications/review/81/05/Classical_May1981.pdf.

*xiv* **"as well as Japan, followed Britain and the US..."** Kris James Mitchener, Masato Shizume, Marc Weidenmier, "Why Did Countries Adopt the Gold Standard? Lessons from Japan," National Bureau of Economic Research Working Paper, July 2009, 24, https://www.nber.org/system/files/working_papers/w15195/w15195.pdf.

*xv* **"Adam Smith observed centuries ago..."** Adam Smith, *The Wealth of Nations,* Adam Smith Institute, https://www.adamsmith.org/the-wealth-of-nations.

*xvii* **"Seven Nobel prizes..."** Brian Domitrovic, "The Economics Nobel Goes to Sargent & Sims: Attackers of the Phillips Curve," *Forbes,* October 10, 2011.

*xvii* **"Had the nation maintained its growth rates..."** Bureau of Economic Analysis, "Table 1.1.1 Percent Change from Preceding Period in Real GDP," https://apps.bea.gov/iTable/index_nipa.cfm.

Bureau of Economic Analysis, "Table 1.1.6 Real Gross Domestic Product, Chained Dollars," https://apps.bea.gov/iTable/index_nipa.cfm.

*xviii* **"Joseph Dodge's..."** *Encyclopedia Britannica,* s.v. "Ikeda Hayato," https://www.britannica.com/biography/Ikeda-Hayato.

CHAPTER ONE:
WHAT IS INFLATION?

1 **"the government issued a $100 *trillion* note..."** "Hyperinflation in Zimbabwe," *Globalization and Monetary Institute 2011 Annual Report,* Federal Reserve Bank of Dallas, 2, https://www.dallasfed.org/~/media/documents/institute/annual/2011/annual11b.pdf.

2 **"Nixon blamed a mild inflation on 'international speculators'..."** Richard Nixon, "Address to the Nation Outlining a New Economic Policy: 'The Challenge of Peace,'" transcript of address delivered in the Oval Office in Washington, DC, August 15, 1971, https://www.presidency.ucsb.edu/documents/address-the-nation-outlining-new-economic-policy-the-challenge-peace.

Kollen Ghizoni, Sandra, "Nixon Ends Convertibility of U.S. Dollars to Gold and Announces Wage/Price Controls," Federal Reserve Bank of St. Louis, August 1971, https://www.federalreservehistory.org/essays/gold-convertibility-ends.

2 **"the monetary principle that the US had embraced..."** Nathan Lewis, *Gold: The Once and Future Money* (Hoboken, John Wiley & Sons, 2007), 31.

3   "dollar's purchasing power has been reduced by 86 percent..."
    "Consumer Price Index, 1913-," Federal Reserve Bank of Minneap-
    olis, https://www.minneapolisfed.org/about-us/monetary-policy/
    inflation-calculator/consumer-price-index-1913-.

3   "In 1970, it took $35 to buy an ounce of gold..." "Historical
    gold charts," Kitco, https://www.kitco.com/charts/historicalgold.
    html.

3   "In the 1960s, oil cost $3 a barrel..." "U.S. Crude Oil First Purchase
    Price," US Energy Information Administration, https://www.eia.gov/
    dnav/pet/hist/LeafHandler.ashx?n=pet&s=f000000___3&f=a.

3   "By mid-2021, oil cost $75 a barrel..." "Cushing, OK WTI Spot
    Price FOB," US Energy Information Administration, https://www.
    eia.gov/dnav/pet/hist/LeafHandler.ashx?n=PET&s=RWTC&f=M.

4   "A Big Mac cost just 65 cents..." Meghan De Maria, "What a Mc-
    Donald's Big Mac Cost the Year You Were Born," Eat This, Not That!,
    November 21, 2020, https://www.eatthis.com/big-mac-cost/.

5   "CPI recorded an increase of 5 percent..." US Bureau of Labor
    Statistics, "Consumer Price Index News Release," https://www.bls.
    gov/news.release/archives/cpi_06102021.htm.

5   "the annual 2 percent rise that the Fed's economists..." "Why
    Does the Federal Reserve Aim for Inflation of 2 Percent Over the
    Longer Run?," Federal Reserve, August 27, 2020, https://www.fed-
    eralreserve.gov/faqs/economy_14400.htm.

5   "According to the Federal Reserve..." "What is Inflation and How
    does the Federal Reserve Measure It?" Federal Reserve, https://www.
    federalreserve.gov/faqs/5CD8134B130A43E998A945450E041BF0.
    htm.

5   "from the authors of the socialist textbook..." William
    Mitchell, L. Randall Wray, Martin Watts, *Macroeconomics* (London:
    Red Globe Press, 2019), 255.

6   "The economist Friedrich Hayek famously explained..."
    Friedrich Hayek, "The Use of Knowledge in Society," *The American
    Economic Review,* XXXV, No. 4., September 1945, 519-30, The Li-
    brary of Economics and Liberty, https://www.econlib.org/library/
    Essays/hykKnw.html.

11  "Experts estimate that..." "Above-Ground Stocks," February
    1, 2021, World Gold Council, https://www.gold.org/goldhub/data/
    above-ground-stocks.

11  **"Alan Greenspan has noted that..."** Alan Greenspan, interview by Steve Forbes, May 11, 2018, raw transcript for *In Money We Trust?* documentary, produced by Our Town Films and BOLDE Communications, distributed by Maryland Public Television, December 29, 2018, film and additional video can be found at https://inmoneywetrust.org/.

12  **"sent the gold price hurtling past $1,900 an ounce..."** "Historical gold charts," Kitco, https://www.kitco.com/charts/historical-gold.html.

13  **"The discount chain Dollar Tree..."** Sarah Nassauer, "How Dollar Tree Sells Nearly Everything for $1, Even when Inflation Lurks," Fox Business, July 12, 2021, https://www.foxbusiness.com/lifestyle/dollar-tree-sales-inflation.

13  **"Eventually the chain was forced to..."** Dollar Tree, "Building on the Success of its 'Combo' Store and Dollar Tree Plus Initiatives, Dollar Tree Poised to Take Next Steps in its Multi-Price Evolution," press release, September 28, 2021, https://www.dollartreeinfo.com/news-releases/news-release-details/building-success-its-combo-store-and-dollar-tree-plus.

13  **"journalist John Steele Gordon issued a warning..."** John Steele Gordon, "Why We're on the Path to a '70s-like Inflation Disaster," *New York Post*, July 12, 2021.

15  **"Bitcoin, for instance, has been known..."** Charles Bovaird, "Bitcoin Lost Roughly 50% of its Value in a Day," *Forbes*, March 12, 2020.

15  **"Platforms such as PayPal..."** Anna Irrera, "Exclusive: PayPal Launches Crypto Checkout Service," Reuters, March 30, 2021, https://www.reuters.com/article/us-crypto-currency-paypal-exclusive/exclusive-paypal-launches-crypto-checkout-service-idUSKBN2BM10N.

15  **"El Salvador, which years ago..."** Nelson Renteria and Anthony Esposito, "El Salvador's World-First Adoption of Bitcoin Endures Bumpy First Day," Reuters, September 8, 2021, https://www.reuters.com/business/finance/el-salvador-leads-world-into-cryptocurrency-bitcoin-legal-tender-2021-09-07/.

## CHAPTER TWO:
## NOT-SO-GREAT MOMENTS IN INFLATION HISTORY

18  **"very first coins, minted in Lydia..."** Nathan Lewis, *Gold: The Once and Future Money* (Hoboken, John Wiley & Sons, 2007), 21.

18  "Nero (37-68 AD)..." *Encyclopedia Britannica,* s.v. "Nero," https://www.britannica.com/biography/Nero-Roman-emperor.

18  "the words of the historian Suetonius..." Fordham University, Ancient History Sourcebook, *Seutonius, De Vita Caesarum—Nero, c. 110 C.E.,* https://sourcebooks.fordham.edu/ancient/suet-nero-rolfe.asp.

18  "Nero debased the Roman denarius..." Lewis, *Gold,* 23.

18  "By 260 AD, Rome's increasingly corrupt governments..." Lewis, *Gold,* 23.

18  "the price of wheat was two million times..." Glyn Davies, *A History of Money: From Ancient Times to the Present Day* (Cardiff: University of Wales Press, 2002).

Adams, Charles, *For Good and Evil: The Impact of Taxes on the Course of Civilization* (Lanham, MD: Madison Books, 1999).

19  "Chinese, meanwhile, were the first to demonstrate the potential..." Lewis, *Gold,* 25-27.

Skeen, Bradley, Penny Morrill, Kenneth Hall, Alan Stahl, and Muhammed Hassan Ali, "Money and coinage," *Encyclopedia of Society and Culture in the Medieval World,* by Pam J. Crabtree, Facts on File, 2008, https://search.credoreference.com/content/entry/fofsociety/money_and_coinage/0?institutionId=10199.

St. Onge, Peter, "How Paper Money Led to the Mongol Conquest," *Independent Review,* Summer 2017, Vol. 22 Issue 2, 223-243, https://www.independent.org/pdf/tir/tir_22_2_09_stonge.pdf.

19  "Around 1440, China returned to highly reliable copper and silver coinage..." Lewis, *Gold,* 27.

19  "Marco Polo returned to Venice in 1295..." Alfred Kennedy, "Marco Polo on Money," Foundation for Economic Freedom, December 1, 1977, https://fee.org/articles/marco-polo-on-money/.

20  "In 1542, he began what was known as the Great Debasement..." Samuel Knafo, *The Making of Modern Finance: Liberal Governance and the Gold Standard* (London: Routledge, 2021), 77-79.

20  "were depleted of about two-thirds of their silver content..." Stephen Deng "The Great Debasement and Its Aftermath," *Coinage and State Formation in Early Modern English Literature,* Early

Modern Cultural Studies, (New York, Palgrave Macmillan, 2011), https://doi.org/10.1057/9780230118249_4.

20　**"sending the price of wheat skyward…"** Margaret Hastings and Michael Charles Prestwich, "England Under the Tudors," *Encyclopedia Britannica*, https://www.britannica.com/place/United-Kingdom.

20　**"Spain's 'silver dollars'…"** Lewis, *Gold*, 56-59, 153.

21　**"royal family itself could not raise the funds to travel…"** J.H. Elliott, *Imperial Spain, 1469-1716* (New York: St. Martin's Press, 1964).

21　**"thanks to his rampant devaluations…"** Elgin Groseclose, "The Great Paper-Money Experiment," *Money and Man* (Norman, OK: University of Oklahoma Press, 1976).

21　**"via the Mississippi Company…"** Jon Moen, "John Law and the Mississippi Bubble: 1718-1720," Mississippi Historical Society, October 2001, https://mshistorynow.mdah.ms.gov/issue/john-law-and-the-mississippi-bubble-1718-1720.

Lewis, *Gold*, 79.

21　**"French stopped using paper money…"** Moen, "John Law."

22　**"In 1690, Massachusetts used paper money…"** Lewis, *Gold*, 153.

22　**"after the American Revolution began in 1775…"** Lewis, *Gold*, 154.

22　**"not worth a Continental…"** "In 1776, the Continental Congress," Cato Institute, https://securessl.cato.org/support/cato1776-coin.

22　**"Paper money also returned with France's Revolution…"** *Encyclopedia Britannica*, s.v. "assignat," https://www.britannica.com/topic/assignat.

22　**"In 1800, a new franc was introduced…"** Lewis, *Gold*, 79-80.

22　**"Alexander Hamilton, the first treasury secretary…"** "Alexander Hamilton (1789-1795)," https://home.treasury.gov/about/history/prior-secretaries/alexander-hamilton-1789-1795.

23　**"the Swiss central bank has had to increase supply…"** "Swiss Franc Stability Not at Risk From Ultra-Loose Policy – SNB," Reuters, October 8, 2020, https://www.reuters.com/article/uk-swiss-snb-jordan/swiss-franc-stability-not-at-risk-from-ultra-loose-policy-snb-idUKKBN26T1JM.

23  **"Between 1775 and 1900, the base money supply..."** Nathan Lewis, "Modern Monetary Theory Goes Mainstream," *Forbes*, July 10, 2020.

24  **"the value of the dollar fell 41 percent..."** Lewis, *Gold,* 229, 231.

24  **"the collapse of the Thai baht and Russian ruble..."** Lewis, *Gold,* 344, 356.

26  **"the South Vietnamese currency, the piastre..."** Wikipedia, s.v. "French Indochinese Piastre," https://en.wikipedia.org/wiki/French_Indochinese_piastre.

"Devalued Piaster is Urged on Saigon," *New York Times*, June 28, 1970, https://www.nytimes.com/1970/06/28/archives/devalued-piaster-is-urged-on-saigon-house-panel-also-suggests-the.html.

26  **"Afghanistan's currency tumbled..."** "Afghanistan's Currency Crumbles to Record Lows," CNN Business, August 18, 2021, https://www.cnn.com/2021/08/18/business/afghanistan-currency-taliban/index.html.

26  **"In 1931, when the Bank of England signaled..."** Ben Bernanke, "Money, Gold, and the Great Depression," Transcript of H. Parker Willis Lecture in Economic Policy, Washington and Lee University, Lexington, VA, March 2, 2004, https://www.federalreserve.gov/boarddocs/speeches/2004/200403022/default.htm.

26  **"a slide in the yen occurred that December..."** Masato Shizume, "The Japanese Economy During the Interwar Period: Instability in the Financial System and the Impact of the World Depression," *Bank of Japan Review,* May 2009, 1, https://www.boj.or.jp/en/research/wps_rev/rev_2009/data/rev09e02.pdf.

26  **"The average budget deficit was 1.3 percent of GDP..."** Office of Management and Budget Historical Tables, The White House, "Table 1.1–Summary of Receipts, Outlays, and Surpluses or Deficits (-): 1789-2026," https://www.whitehouse.gov/omb/historical-tables/.

26  **"The debt-to-GDP ratio was around 35 percent..."** US Office of Management and Budget and Federal Reserve Bank of St. Louis, "Federal Debt: Total Public Debt as Percent of Gross Domestic Product," Federal Reserve Bank of St. Louis (FRED), https://fred.stlouisfed.org/series/GFDEGDQ188S.

27  **"Between 1970 and 1974, the number of dollars..."** "Historical Gold Charts," Kitco, https://www.kitco.com/charts/historicalgold.html.

27  **"The monetary base…"** Board of Governors of the Federal Reserve System, "Monetary Base; Total," Federal Reserve Bank of St. Louis (FRED), https://fred.stlouisfed.org/series/BOGMBASE.

27  **"dollar base money supply did increase by 51 percent…"** FRED, "Monetary Base."

27  **"The quadrupling of oil prices in 1973-74…"** Michael Corbett, "Oil Shock of 1973-74," Federal Reserve Bank of St. Louis, January 1974, https://www.federalreservehistory.org/essays/oil-shock-of-1973-74.

27  **"Currency expert Steve Hanke defines hyperinflation as…"** Steve Hanke, "Hanke's Inflation Dashboard: The Media's Misreporting on Hyperinflation," Cato Institute, October 7, 2020, https://www.cato.org/commentary/hankes-inflation-dashboard-medias-misreporting-hyperinflation.

28  **"the European allies demanded the nation pay war reparations in the Treaty of Versailles of 1919…"** United States Holocaust Memorial Museum, *Holocaust Encyclopedia*, s.v. "Treaty of Versailles," https://encyclopedia.ushmm.org/content/en/article/treaty-of-versailles.

28  **"Between January 1919 and February 1920, the monetary base increased by 58 percent…"** "Changes in Base Money Demand in Germany," *New World Economics*, February 27, 2011.

29  **"people bought pianos who couldn't play them…"** Adam Fergusson, *When Money Dies* (London: Kimber, 1975), 64.

29  **"an astonishing level of nearly 30,000 percent *per month*…"** Rudiger Dornbusch, "Stopping Hyperinflation: Lessons from the German Inflation Experience of the 1920s," National Bureau of Economic Research Working Paper, August 1985, https://www.nber.org/system/files/working_papers/w1675/w1675.pdf.

29  **"In Fergusson's words…"** Adam Fergusson, interview by Steve Forbes, June 5, 2018, raw transcript for *In Money We Trust?* documentary, produced by Our Town Films and BOLDE Communications, distributed by Maryland Public Television, December 29, 2018, film and additional video can be found at https://inmoneywetrust.org/.

29  **"In November 1923, the old currency was thrown out…"** Fergusson, *When Money Dies,* 120-122.

"In Hyperinflation's Aftermath, How Germany Went Back to Gold," *Forbes*, June 9, 2011.

Polleit, Thorsten, "90 Years Ago: The End of German Hyperinflation," Mises Institute, November 15, 2013, https://mises.org/library/90-years-ago-end-german-hyperinflation.

30  **"In 1922, 63 percent of the nation's total government spending…"** Costantino Bresciani-Turroni, *The Economics of Inflation–A Study of Currency Depreciation in Post War Germany* (London: G. Allen & Unwin Ltd., 1937).

31  **"Franklin Roosevelt took office in 1933, he devalued…"** "Gold Standard Dropped for the Present to Lift Prices and Aid Our Trade Position; Plans for Controlled Inflation Drafted," *New York Times,* April 20, 1933.

Lewis, *Gold, 229.*

31  **"John Maynard Keynes rose to prominence…"** Christina Romer, *Encyclopedia Britannica,* s.v. "Great Depression," https://www.britannica.com/event/Great-Depression.

Jahan, Sarwat, Ahmed Saber Mahmud, and Chris Papageorgiou, "What is Keynesian Economics?," *Finance & Development,* September 2014, Vol. 51, No. 3, 53-54, International Monetary Fund, https://www.imf.org/external/pubs/ft/fandd/2014/09/basics.htm.

32  **"New Zealand economist William Phillips came up with the Phillips Curve…"** James Dorn, "The Phillips Curve: A Poor Guide for Monetary Policy," Cato Institute, Winter 2020, https://www.cato.org/cato-journal/winter-2020/phillips-curve-poor-guide-monetary-policy.

32  **"led President Richard Nixon, and his Fed Chair Arthur Burns…"** Alan Reynolds, "The Fed: Lessons of 1972," Cato Institute, May 13, 2004, https://www.cato.org/publications/commentary/fed-lessons-1972#.

32  **"Phillips Curve was disproved by a succession of Nobel-prize winning economists…"** Brian Domitrovic, "Nobel After Nobel Won't Kill the Phillips Curve," *Forbes,* March 7, 2011, https://www.forbes.com/sites/briandomitrovic/2011/03/07/nobel-after-nobelwont-kill-the-phillips-curve/?sh=45935be52f53.

32  **"The original mandate of this new entity…"** David Wheelock and Mark Carlson, "The Fed's First (and Lasting) Job: Lender of Last Resort," *Forefront,* June 26, 2013, https://www.clevelandfed.org/en/newsroom-and-events/publications/forefront/ff-v4n01/ff-v4n0108-the-feds-first-job-lender-of-last-resort.aspx.

33 **"The Employment Act of 1946..."** Aaron Steelman, "Employment Act of 1946," Federal Reserve Bank of St. Louis, https://www.federalreservehistory.org/essays/employment-act-of-1946.

33 **"In the late 1970s, Congress required the Federal Reserve..."** Robert Hetzel, "Money, Banking, and Monetary Policy From the Formation of the Federal Reserve Until Today," Working Paper 16-01, Federal Reserve Bank of Richmond, 25, https://fraser.stlouisfed.org/title/working-papers-federal-reserve-bank-richmond-3942/money-banking-monetary-policy-formation-federal-reserve-to-day-531445.

33 **"that are the 'primary dealers' of those securities..."** "Primary Dealers," Federal Reserve Bank of New York, https://www.newyorkfed.org/markets/primarydealers.

34 **"Judy Shelton observes in the *Wall Street Journal*..."** Judy Shelton, "How the Fed Finances U.S. Debt," *Wall Street Journal,* October 13, 2021.

36 **"a speech in 2012, then Fed Chair Ben Bernanke explained..."** Ben Bernanke, "Monetary Policy Since the Onset of the Crisis," Transcript of Speech delivered to the Federal Reserve Bank of Kansas City Economic Symposium, Jackson Hole, Wyoming, August 31, 2012, https://www.federalreserve.gov/newsevents/speech/bernanke20120831a.htm.

36 **"Some central banks, notably in Japan and Switzerland..."** Hideyuki Sano, "BOJ Buys Stock ETFs as Usual After Policy Change, But Changes May Lie Ahead," Reuters, March 22, 2021, https://www.reuters.com/article/us-japan-boj-stocks/boj-buys-stock-etfs-as-usual-after-policy-change-but-changes-may-lie-ahead-idUSKBN2BE17M.

Sugiyama, Kentaro, and Leika Kihara, "Take On More Risk or Taper? BOJ Faces Tough Choice with REIT Buying," Reuters, March 4, 2021, https://www.reuters.com/article/us-japan-boj-reit/take-on-more-risk-or-taper-boj-faces-tough-choice-with-reit-buying-idUSKBN2AW0ND.

Bosley, Catherine, "Swiss Central Bank Owns Record $162 Billion of U.S. Stocks," *Bloomberg*, August 6, 2021, https://www.bloomberg.com/news/articles/2021-08-06/swiss-central-bank-s-hoard-of-foreign-exchange-tops-1-trillion.

37 **"ran the largest peacetime deficits ever..."** Office of Management and Budget, "Table 1.1–Summary of Receipts, Outlays, and Surpluses or Deficits (-): 1789-2026," https://www.whitehouse.gov/omb/historical-tables/.

37  "new global banking regulations under the 'Basel III'..." Basel Committee on Banking Supervision, Bank for International Settlements, "Finalising Basel III, In Brief," December 2017, https://www.bis.org/bcbs/publ/d424_inbrief.pdf.

37  "the Fed, in another unprecedented move, started paying interest..." Federal Reserve, "Interest on Reserve Balances," https://www.federalreserve.gov/monetarypolicy/reserve-balances.htm.

37  "James Grant, editor of *Grant's Interest Rate Observer*..." James Grant, interview by Steve Forbes, May 2 2018, raw transcript for *In Money We Trust?* documentary, produced by Our Town Films and BOLDE Communications, distributed by Maryland Public Television, December 29, 2018, film and additional video can be found at https://inmoneywetrust.org/.

37  "Between 2008 and early 2021, the US monetary base—currency in circulation and bank reserves— exploded..." Board of Governors of the Federal Reserve System (US), "Monetary Base; Total," Federal Reserve Bank of St. Louis (FRED), https://fred.stlouisfed.org/series/BOGMBASE.

38  "Between 2008 and 2020, the value of the dollar fell in half..." "Historical gold charts," Kitco, https://www.kitco.com/charts/historicalgold.html.

38  "In 2021, the Fed was still buying $120 billion in Treasuries..." Federal Reserve, Press release, July 28, 2021, https://www.federalreserve.gov/monetarypolicy/files/monetary20210728a1.pdf.

38  "something called a 'reverse repurchase agreement'..." Federal Reserve, "Factors Affecting Reserve Balances – H.4.1," https://www.federalreserve.gov/releases/h41/.

Federal Reserve Bank of New York, "FAQs: Reverse Repurchase Agreement Operations," September 22, 2021, https://www.newyorkfed.org/markets/rrp_faq.html.

Chen, James, "Reverse Repurchase Agreement," Investopedia, December 28, 2020, https://www.investopedia.com/terms/r/reverserepurchaseagreement.asp.

39  "In February of 2021, the Fed had very few reverse repos..." Federal Reserve, "Factors Affecting Reserve Balances – H.4.1," February 25, 2021, https://www.federalreserve.gov/releases/h41/20210225/.

39  "swelled to more than $1.7 trillion..." Federal Reserve, "Factors

Affecting Reserve Balances–H.4.1," December 23, 2021, https://www.federalreserve.gov/releases/h41/20211223/.

40    **"publication of *The Deficit Myth*..."** Stephanie Kelton, *The Deficit Myth: Modern Monetary Theory and the Birth of the People's Economy* (New York: Public Affairs, 2020).

40    **"twice the percentage of US federal debt..."** US Department of the Treasury, Fiscal Service, "Federal Debt Held by Federal Reserve Banks," Federal Reserve Bank of St. Louis (FRED), https://fred.stlouisfed.org/series/FDHBFRBN.

CHAPTER THREE:
WHY INFLATION IS BAD

42    **"The famed 'WIN' button..."** Courtesy of the Gerald R. Ford Presidential Museum via Wikimedia Commons.

43    **"Federal Reserve Chair Jerome Powell announced..."** Jerome Powell, "New Economic Challenges and the Fed's Monetary Policy Review," transcript of speech delivered to the economic policy symposium sponsored by the Federal Reserve Bank of Kansas City, August 27, 2020, https://www.federalreserve.gov/newsevents/speech/powell20200827a.htm.

44    **"lack of inflation can create problems for consumers..."** Mitchell Hartman, "I've Always Wondered . . .Why is Inflation Necessary?," Marketplace, September 12, 2019, https://www.marketplace.org/2019/09/12/why-is-inflation-necessary/.

44    **"median household income grew by 6.8 percent..."** Editorial, "The Higher Wages of Growth," *Wall Street Journal,* September 16, 2020.

44    **"The *New York Times* applauded..."** Binyamin Appelbaum, "In Fed and Out, Many Now Think Inflation Helps," *New York Times,* October 26, 2013.

44    **"We wonder if anyone cared to ask Richard Dixson..."** Gerald Porter, Jr., "Diaper Inflation Wrecks Already-Strained Family Budgets in the U.S.," Bloomberg, July 9, 2021, https://www.bloomberg.com/news/articles/2021-07-09/diaper-costs-crush-families-as-p-g-and-kimberly-clark-pass-along-inflation.

45    **"Melissa Roberts, a young mother of four..."** Elisabeth Buchwald, "Eggs and Pancakes for Dinner: How One Family of Seven Is Coping with America's Food Inflation," MarketWatch, updated

July 19, 2021, https://www.marketwatch.com/story/eggs-and-pan-cakes-for-dinner-how-one-family-of-seven-is-coping-with-americas-food-inflation-11626285167.

45 **"Cambodia, where upwardly spiraling food prices . . ."** UNICEF, "Going hungry–how COVID-19 has harmed nutrition in Asia and the Pacific," press release, February 1, 2021, https://www.unicef.org/cambodia/press-releases/going-hungry-how-covid-19-has-harmed-nutrition-asia-and-pacific.

45 **"John Maynard Keynes first advanced the notion . . ."** Sarwat Jahan, Ahmed Saber Mahmud, and Chris Papageorgiou, "What is Keynesian Economics?," *Finance & Development*, Vol. 51, No. 3, September 2014, International Monetary Fund, https://www.imf.org/external/pubs/ft/fandd/2014/09/basics.htm.

46 **"Seven Nobel prizes have been awarded . . ."** Brian Domitrovic, interview by Steve Forbes, May 23, 2018, raw transcript for *In Money We Trust?* documentary, produced by Our Town Films and BOLDE Communications, distributed by Maryland Public Television, December 29, 2018, film and additional video can be found at https://inmoneywetrust.org/.

46 **"During the inflationary early 1980s . . ."** Brian Domitrovic, "The Fed is Failing its Unemployment Mandate," *Forbes*, September 20, 2011.

Domitrovic, Brian "We're Learning from the 1980s/Push for Gold, At Last," *Forbes*, January 24, 2012.

46 **"jobless rates of less than 5 percent . . ."** Stanley Lebergott, "Annual Estimates of Unemployment in the United States, 1900-1954," *The Measurement and Behavior of Unemployment* (Washington, DC: National Bureau of Economic Research, 1957) 211, 242.

46 **"and the 1960s . . ."** US Bureau of Labor Statistics, "Unemployment Rate," Federal Reserve Bank of St. Louis (FRED), https://fred.stlouisfed.org/series/UNRATE.

46 **"Switzerland [. . .] unemployment rate hovers around 3 percent . . ."** Organization for Economic Co-operation and Development, "Registered Unemployment Rate for Switzerland," Federal Reserve Bank of St. Louis (FRED), https://fred.stlouisfed.org/series/LMUNRRTTCHQ156S.

47 **"the US during the late nineteenth-century . . ."** "Deflation and Economic Growth," *National Economic Trends,* March 1998.

47 **"Cheap steel poured into new railways…"** Nathan Lewis, *Gold: The Final Standard* (New Berlin, NY: Canyon Maple Publishing 2017) 134.

47 **"more than 7,000 miles of new railway per year…"** National Bureau of Economic Research, "Miles of Railroad Built for United States," Federal Reserve Bank of St. Louis (FRED), https://fred.stlouisfed.org/series/A02F2AUSA374NNBR.

47 **"In the 1850s, whale oil…"** Paul Robinson, "Petroleum and Its Products," *Handbook of Industrial Chemistry and Biotechnology* (Springer US, November 2012), 699-747, https://www.researchgate.net/publication/302207461_Petroleum_and_Its_Products.

Robbins, James, "How Capitalism Saved the Whales," Foundation for Economic Education, August 1, 1992, https://fee.org/articles/how-capitalism-saved-the-whales/.

47 **"kerosene replaced whale oil at $0.26 per gallon…"** Burton Folsom, "John D. Rockefeller and the Oil Industry," Foundation for Economic Education, October 1, 1988, https://fee.org/articles/john-d-rockefeller-and-the-oil-industry/.

48 **"In the words of Steve Hanke…"** Steve Hanke, interview by Steve Forbes, April 17, 2018, raw transcript for *In Money We Trust?* documentary, produced by Our Town Films and BOLDE Communications, distributed by Maryland Public Television, December 29, 2018, film and additional video can be found at https://inmoneywetrust.org/.

48 **"Former congressman Ron Paul…"** Steve Forbes and Elizabeth Ames, *Money: How The Destruction of the Dollar Threatens the Global Economy—and What We Can Do About It*, (New York: McGraw Hill Education, 2014), 81.

48 **"Keynes himself famously acknowledged…"** John Maynard Keynes, *The Economic Consequences of the Peace* (New York: Harcourt, Brace, and Howe, 1920), chapter 6.

49 **"Stony Brook University professor and social scientist…"** Todd Pittinsky, "Inflation Disproportionately Hurts the Poor," (letter) *Wall Street Journal*, June 20, 2021.

49 **"Noted economist and author Mark Skousen…"** Mark Skousen, interview by Steve Forbes, Jun 18, 2018, raw transcript for *In Money We Trust?* documentary, produced by Our Town Films and BOLDE Communications, distributed by Maryland Public Television, December 29, 2018, film and additional video can be found at https://inmoneywetrust.org/.

50 **"2021 saw the biggest one-year increase in federal tax receipts..."** Brian Faler, "U.S. Sees Biggest Revenue Surge in 44 Years Despite Pandemic," *Politico*, October 12, 2021.

50 **"in October of 2021, the *Wall Street Journal* reported..."** Editorial, "The Inflation Tax Rises: Real Average Hourly Earnings Have Declined 1.9% Since Biden's Inaugural," *Wall Street Journal*, October 13, 2021.

50 **"According to eye-opening calculations..."** Zheli He and Xiaoyue Sun, "Impact of Inflation by Household Income," Penn Wharton Budget Model, December 15, 2021, https://budgetmodel.wharton. upenn.edu/issues/2021/12/15/consumption-under-inflation-costs

50 **"John Locke [...] currency devaluation a 'public failure of justice'..."** John Locke, *The Works of John Locke*, vol. 5 (London: Thomas Davison, Whitefriars, 1823), 145.

50 **"In 2021, Argentina had an annual inflation rate..."** Herman Nessi and Jorge Lorio, "Argentina's Annual Inflation Rate Tops 50% as Global Prices Soar," Reuters, July 15, 2021, https://www.reuters. com/world/americas/argentina-inflation-seen-year-low-32-june-likely-reheat-2nd-half-2021-07-15/.

51 **"Turkey, which had a more moderate inflation rate..."** Reuters Graphics, "Turkish inflation jumps above policy rate," https:// graphics.reuters.com/TURKEYECONOMY/INFLATION/jbyvrzxj-dve/index.html.

51 **"In the US during the inflationary 1970s..."** Board of Governors of the Federal Reserve System (US), "Bank Prime Loan Rate Changes: Historical Dates of Changes and Rates [PRIME]," Federal Reserve Bank of St. Louis (FRED), https://fred.stlouisfed.org/series/PRIME.

51 **"pushed interest rates down to some of the lowest levels..."** "What are negative interest rates and how would they affect me?," Bank of England, updated September 10, 2021, https://www. bankofengland.co.uk/knowledgebank/what-are-negative-interest-rates.

52 **"The computer giant Apple..."** Chuck Jones, "Apple Will Have to Buyback $250 Billion in Stock to Become Cash Neutral," *Forbes*, February 28, 2021,

52 **"total federal debt in early 2021..."** US Department of the Treasury, Fiscal Service, "Federal Debt: Total Public Debt," Federal Reserve Bank of St. Louis (FRED), https://fred.stlouisfed.org/series/GFDEBTN.

52 **"Johns Hopkins political scientist..."** Josef Joffe, "America Looks More Like Europe All the Time," *Wall Street Journal*, August 22, 2021.

53 **"From 1973 to 1975, oil rose from its longtime level..."** Federal Bank of St. Louis, "Spot Crude Oil Price: West Texas Intermediate (WTI)," Federal Reserve Bank of St. Louis (FRED), https://fred.stlouisfed.org/series/WTISPLC.

53 ***Newsweek* declared in a cover story..."** Nathan Lewis, "Commodities in the 1970s," New World Economics, April 1, 2007, https://newworldeconomics.com/commodities-in-the-1970s/.

53 **"was a currency crisis, not an oil crisis..."** Brian Domitrovic, interview by Steve Forbes, May 23, 2018, raw transcript for *In Money We Trust?* documentary, produced by Our Town Films and BOLDE Communications, distributed by Maryland Public Television, December 29, 2018, film and additional video can be found at https://inmoneywetrust.org/.

53 **"He points to a letter from the secretary general of OPEC..."** Brian Domitrovic, "Oil Soared Because the U.S. Tanked the Dollar," *Forbes*, May 8, 2018.

53 **"would not have exceeded fifty cents..."** Domitrovic interview, May 23, 2018.

54 **"the Fed [...] lowered the federal funds rate..."** Board of Governors of the Federal Reserve System, "Federal Funds Effective Rate," Federal Reserve Bank of St. Louis (FRED), https://fred.stlouisfed.org/series/FEDFUNDS.

54 **"Between 2000 and 2003 the monetary base grew..."** Board of Governors of the Federal Reserve System, "Monetary Base; Total", Federal Reserve Bank of St. Louis (FRED), https://fred.stlouisfed.org/series/BOGMBASE.

54 **"gold moved sharply upward..."** "Historical gold charts," Kitco, https://www.kitco.com/charts/historicalgold.html.

54 **"subprime mortgage market grew by 200 percent..."** Charles Schumer and Carolyn Maloney, "The Subprime Lending Crisis," Report and Recommendations by the Majority Staff of the Joint Economic Committee, October 2007, https://www.jec.senate.gov/archive/Documents/Reports/10.25.07OctoberSubprimeReport.pdf.

54 **" 'Stated income loans' became common..."** The Financial Crisis Inquiry Commission, "The Financial Crisis Inquiry Report: Final Report of the National Commission on the Causes of the Financial

and Economic Crisis in the United States," January 2011, https://
www.govinfo.gov/content/pkg/GPO-FCIC/pdf/GPO-FCIC.pdf.

54 **"A homeless man in St. Petersburg..."** Jeff Testerman, "Investor, or
Pauper or Merely a Front Man?," *Tampa Bay Times*, April 9, 2006.

55 **"In 2005, the Fed started to raise interest rates..."** Testerman,
"Investor, or Pauper."

55 **"10 million people were said to have lost their homes..."**
William Emmons, "The End is in Sight for the U.S. Foreclosure
Crisis," On The Economy Blog, December 2, 2016, https://www.
stlouisfed.org/on-the-economy/2016/december/end-sight-us-fore-
closure-crisis#endnote1.

55 **"investment houses Lehman Brothers and Bear Stearns..."**
Federal Deposit Insurance Corporation, "Crisis and Response: An
FDIC History, 2008–2013," https://www.fdic.gov/bank/historical/
crisis/overview.pdf.

55 **"The S&P 500 stock index saw a 58 percent drop..."** Investopedia, s.v. "What is the History of the S&P 500?," updated October 26, 2021, https://www.investopedia.com/ask/answers/041015/
what-history-sp-500.asp.

56 **"you had a brick account..."** Steve Hanke, interview by Steve
Forbes, April 17, 2018, raw transcript for *In Money We Trust?* documentary, produced by Our Town Films and BOLDE Communications, distributed by Maryland Public Television, December 29,
2018, film and additional video can be found at https://inmoney-
wetrust.org/.

56 **"'inflationary adjustments,' which were introduced in the
1980s..."** Alex Muresianu and Jason Harrison, "How the Tax Code
Handles Inflation (and How It Doesn't)," Tax Foundation, June 28,
2021, https://taxfoundation.org/taxes-inflation/.

56 **"A family of four making twice the median income..."** US
Census Bureau, "Consumer Income," *Current Population Reports,*
Series P-60, No. 49, August 10, 1966, https://www2.census.gov/
prod2/popscan/p60-049.pdf.

56 **"had a marginal tax rate of 25 percent in 1965..."** Tax Foundation,
"Federal Individual Income Tax Rates History," https://files.taxfounda-
tion.org/legacy/docs/fed_individual_rate_history_nominal.pdf.

56 **"rose to 43 percent..."** US Census Bureau, "Money Income of
Households, Families, and Persons in the United States:1980," Re-

port Number P60-132, July 1982, https://www.census.gov/library/publications/1982/demo/p60-132.html.

57 **"During the 1970s, the *real* tax on capital gains..."** Stephen Entin, "Getting 'Real' by Indexing Capital Gains for Inflation," Tax Foundation, March 6, 2018, https://taxfoundation.org/inflation-adjusting-capital-gains/.

57 **"if you had bought an S&P 500 index fund in 1970..."** Nathan Lewis's calculations based on data from Measuring Worth, https://www.measuringworth.com.

57 **"tax shelters of just about every kind proliferated..."** Robert Hershey, Jr., "The Boom in Tax Shelters," *New York Times,* July 19,1983, Section D, 1.

58 **"Initial Public Offerings (IPOs) went from nearly..."** "Revenue Proposals Contained in the President's Budget for Fiscal Year 1990," Vol 4, p 15, https://books.google.com/books?id=36-jxgEACAA-J&q=Initial+Public+Offerings#v=snippet&q=Initial%20Public%20Offerings&f=false.

58 **"Peruvians who started building new houses..."** "What's with All the Unfinished Buildings in Peru and Boliva?," Overland Traveler's Blog, December 13, 2009, https://overlandtraveller.wordpress.com/2009/12/13/what's-with-all-the-unfinished-buildings-in-peru-and-bolivia/.

58 **"Torre de David..."** Simon Romero and María Díaz, "A 45-Story Walkup Beckons the Desperate," *New York Times*, March 1, 2011.

59 **"between 1950 and 1970, real GDP per capita grew..."** Bureau of Economic Analysis, "Table 7.1 Selected Per Capita Product and Income Series in Current and Chained Dollars," https://apps.bea.gov/iTable/iTable.cfm?reqid=19&step=2#reqid=19&step=2&isuri=1&1921=survey.

World Bank, "GDP Per Capita Growth (annual %) - United States," https://data.worldbank.org/indicator/NY.GDP.PCAP.KD.ZG?locations=US.

59 **"average American is more than twice as wealthy as in 1970..."** US Bureau of Economic Analysis, "Real Gross Domestic Product Per Capita," Federal Reserve Bank of St. Louis (FRED), https://fred.stlouisfed.org/series/A939RX0Q048SBEA.

60 **"In ancient Rome, the Emperor Diocletian..."** Bruce Bartlett, "The Futility of Price Controls," *Forbes*, January 15, 2010,

61   **"more than 200,000 new rules have been added..."** James Copland, *The Unelected: How an Unaccountable Elite is Governing America* (New York: Encounter Books, 2020), 19.

61   **"but 98 percent of these were never voted on by Congress..."** Copland, *The Unelected,* 19.

61   **"The CDC's 'eviction moratoria'..."** United State Supreme Court, "Alabama Association of Realtors, et al. v. Department of Health and Human Services, et al. on Application to Vacate Stay," No. 21A23, 594 U.S. (2021), https://www.supremecourt.gov/opinions/20pdf/21a23_ap6c.pdf.

61   **"acute dependency on government programs..."** George Gilder, *The Scandal of Money: Why Wall Street Recovers but the Economy Never Does* (Washington, DC: Regnery Gateway, 2016), 16.

62   **"There is no subtler, no surer means..."** John Maynard Keynes, *Economic Consequences of Peace* (New York: Harcourt, Brace, and Howe, 1920), 236.

63   **"The Romans in the third century blamed the Christians..."** Steve Forbes and Elizabeth Ames, *MONEY,* 109.

63   **"Something must be treated in such a way..."** Elias Canetti, *Crowds and Power*, translated from the German by Carol Stewart, (New York: Continuum, 1962), 187.

64   **"Getting ahead seems impossible..."** Nicholas Engelmann, "Argentina's Inflation Problem, and How It's Permeated Every Aspect of the Culture," *Paste*, December 7, 2016.

64   **"As the old virtues of thrift, honesty, and hard work..."** Adam Fergusson, *When Money Dies: The Nightmare of the Weimar Collapse* (London: William Kimber & Co. Ltd., 1975), 229.

64   **"There were few in any class of society..."** Fergusson, *When Money Dies,* 236.

65   **"Venezuela, where the annual inflation rate..."** Colin Dwyer, "Venezuela, Racked With Hyperinflation, Rolls Out New Banknotes," NPR.org, August 20, 2018, https://www.npr.org/2018/08/20/640213152/venezuela-racked-with-hyperinflation-rolls-out-new-banknotes.

65   **"highest crime rate of any nation in South America..."** "Venezuela 2020 Crime and Safety Report," Overseas Security Advisory Council, July 21, 2020, https://www.osac.gov/Country/

Venezuela/Content/Detail/Report/0e6ed0e0-eb8e-44cc-ab81-1938e6c8d93f.

65 **"linking inflation to crime..."** Jen Hatton, "Criminologist Discusses Inflation's Effect on Crime," UMSL Daily, September 20, 2011, https://blogs.umsl.edu/news/2011/09/20/crimerates/.

66 **"The 2010 Tunisian street demonstrations..."** *Encyclopedia Britannica*, s.v. "Jasmine Revolution," https://www.britannica.com/event/Jasmine-Revolution.

66 **"Egypt, where the consumer price index had jumped to 18 percent..."** The World Bank, "Inflation, Consumer Prices, Egypt, Arab Rep.," https://data.worldbank.org/indicator/FP.CPI.TOTL.ZG?locations=EG.

66 **"Iran, where inflation surged to an official rate of 25 percent..."** The World Bank, "Inflation, Consumer Prices, Iran, Islamic Rep.," https://data.worldbank.org/indicator/FP.CPI.TOTL.ZG?locations=IR.

66 **"In 1989, a hyperinflation began in Russia..."** Nathan Lewis, *Gold: The Once and Future Money* (New York: Wiley, 2007), 81, 378.

66 **"Indonesia suffered price rises..."** Lewis, *Gold*, 81.

66 **"Yugoslavia suffered a hyperinflation..."** Lewis, *Gold*, 81.

Lampe, J.R., and John Allcock, "Yugoslavia," *Encyclopedia Britannica*, https://www.britannica.com/place/Yugoslavia-former-federated-nation-1929-2003.

66 **"In the 1790s, a hyperinflation in revolutionary France..."** Richard Ebeling, "The Great French Inflation," Foundation for Economic Education, July 1, 2007.

66 **"Napoleon, who stabilized the currency..."** Nathan Lewis, *Gold: The Final Standard* (New Berlin, NY: Canyon Maple Publishing, 2019), 79-80.

67 **"former Fed Chair Paul Volcker warned of the dangers..."** Paul Volcker, interview by Steve Forbes, May 10, 2018, raw transcript for *In Money We Trust?* documentary, produced by Our Town Films and BOLDE Communications, distributed by Maryland Public Television, December 29, 2018, film and additional video can be found at https://inmoneywetrust.org/.

67 **"By late 2021, Volcker's prediction had come true..."** Bureau

of Labor Statistics, "Consumer Price Index-October 2021," November 10, 2021, "https://www.bls.gov/news.release/cpi.nr0.htm.

67 **"trust in American political institutions has plunged..."** Pew Research Center, "Public Trust in Government: 1958-2021," May 17, 2021, https://www.pewresearch.org/politics/2021/05/17/public-trust-in-government-1958-2021/.

68 **"Biden administration blaming meat producers..."** Will Feuer, "White House Blames Big Meat for Rising Prices, Alleges 'Profiteering,'" *New York Post,* September 9, 2021.

68 **"Russia felt free to march into Afghanistan in December 1979..."** *Encyclopedia Britannica,* s.v. "Soviet Invasion of Afghanistan," https://www.britannica.com/event/Soviet-invasion-of-Afghanistan/.

## CHAPTER FOUR:
### HOW TO END THE MALAISE

70 **"Argentina has periodically restricted companies from doing business in dollars..."** "Argentina Imposes Currency Controls to Support Economy," BBC News, September 2, 2019.

70 **"The use of credit cards has been limited..."** João Paulo Pimentel, Luciana Rosa, Reuters, "Argentina's Tightened Currency Rules Affect Dollar-Denominated Card Purchases," Latin America Business Stories, September 17, 2020.

70 **"The value of the Argentine peso..."** "US Dollar to Argentine Peso Exchange Rate Chart," XE, https://www.xe.com/currency-charts/?from=USD&to=ARS&view=5Y.

70 **"a sliding Turkish lira..."** "US Dollar to Turkish Lira Exchange Rate Chart," XE, https://www.xe.com/currencycharts/?from=USD&to=TRY&view=10Y.

70 **"blaming foreign 'food terrorists'..."** Ragip Soylu, "Turkey Cracks Down on 'Food Terrorism' with Government Shops," *Middle East Eye,* February 12, 2019.

70 **"Food prices continue to rise by more than 25 percent annually..."** Azra Ceylan and Jonathan Spicer, "Turkey to Open 1,000 markets to Counter High Inflation, Erdogan says," Reuters, October 3, 2021, https://www.reuters.com/world/middle-east/turkey-open-1000-new-markets-counter-inflation-erdogan-says-2021-10-03/.

70   **"With an inflation rate that's the highest in the world, Venezuela..."** Aaron O'Neill, "The 20 Countries with the Highest Inflation Rate in 2020," Statista, June 16, 2021, https://www.statista.com/statistics/268225/countries-with-the-highest-inflation-rate/.

70   **"price controls on everything from corn flour and car parts..."** Kejal Veyas, "Venezuela Quietly Loosens Grip on Market, Tempering Economic Crisis," *Wall Street Journal,* September 17, 2019.

71   **"Richard Nixon responded with a ninety-day freeze..."** Sandra Kollen Ghizoni, "Nixon Ends Convertibility of U.S. Dollars to Gold and Announces Wage/Price Controls," Federal Reserve Bank of St. Louis, August 1971, https://www.federalreservehistory.org/essays/gold-convertibility-ends.

71   **"He later instituted a Pay Board and Price Commission..."** Gene Healy, "Remembering Nixon's Wage and Price Controls," Cato Institute, August 16, 2011, https://www.cato.org/commentary/remembering-nixons-wage-price-controls.

71   **"Gerald Ford, responded to upwardly spiraling oil prices..."** Gerald Ford, "Remarks to the Annual Convention of the Future Farmers of America, Kansas City, Missouri," The American Presidency Project, October 15, 1974, https://www.presidency.ucsb.edu/documents/remarks-the-annual-convention-the-future-farmers-america-kansas-city-missouri.

71   **"big red buttons with the acronym 'WIN'..."** Ford Library Museum, "Whip Inflation Now (WIN)," https://www.fordlibrarymuseum.gov/museum/artifactcollectionsamples/win.html.

72   **"In a famous speech, while wearing a cardigan sweater..."** "Jimmy Carter's First Report to the American People," *New York Times,* February 3, 1977.

72   **"the inflation rate, which reached nearly 15 percent..."** Michael Bryan, "The Great Inflation 1965—1982," Federal Reserve Bank of St. Louis, November 22, 2013, https://www.federalreservehistory.org/essays/great-inflation.

73   **"International Monetary Fund (IMF), the global organization..."** International Monetary Fund, "The IMF at a Glance," March 3, 2021, https://www.imf.org/en/About/Factsheets/IMF-at-a-Glance.

73   **"The IMF's Bad Medicine in Asia..."** Nathan Lewis, *Gold: The Once and Future Money* (New York: Wiley, 2007), 341–373.

74   **"A Russian Currency Disaster..."** Lewis, *Gold,* 378–382.

76 **"Black-market currency traders known as *arbolitos*..."** Joan Manuel Santiago Lopez, "Argentina's 'Little Trees' Blossom as Forex Controls Fuel Black Market," Reuters, February 5, 2020. https://www.reuters.com/article/us-argentina-currency-blackmarket/argentinas-little-trees-blossom-as-forex-controls-fuel-black-market-idUSKBN1ZZ1H1.

77 **"Thailand and South Korea, to cite just two examples..."** Lewis, *Gold,* 350.

78 **"can come with countless requirements..."** Lewis, *Gold,* 354.

78 **"The only thing that did work, temporarily..."** Steve Hanke, "On the Fall of the Rupiah and Suharto," Cato Institute, January 27, 2007, https://www.cato.org/publications/commentary/fall-rupiah-suharto.

78 **"The rupiah collapsed again..."** "Professor Hanke vs. the IMF," *Johns Hopkins Magazine,* June 1998.

80 **"Cigarettes and chocolate circulated as money..."** Lewis, *Gold,* 42, 384.

81 **"Ludwig Erhard, took the opposite of the austerity approach..."** Isabella Weber, "How to Make a Miracle? Ludwig Erhard's Post-War Price Liberalisation in China's 1980s Reform Debate," Working Paper, Dept. of Economics, New School for Social Research, March 2019, http://www.economicpolicyresearch.org/econ/2019/NSSR_WP_032019.pdf.

81 **"The top income tax rate fell from 95 percent to 53 percent..."** "Individual Income Tax Rates in West German, 1946-66," *Reason,* https://reason.com/wp-content/uploads/assets/db/15402236542664.pdf.

81 **"Dodge again imposed..."** Nathan Lewis, "It's Time to Plan for the Post-Crisis World," New World Economics, April 24, 2020, https://newworldeconomics.com/its-time-to-plan-for-the-post-crisis-world/.

81 **"Like Germany, Japan reduced its taxes dramatically..."** Lewis, *Gold,* 43, 322-326.

82 **"By the end of the decade, inflation had reached nearly 15 percent..."** Bryan, "The Great Inflation."

82 **"Enter Paul Volcker..."** Board of Governors, "Paul A. Volcker," Federal Reserve Bank of St. Louis, https://www.federalreservehistory.org/people/paul-a-volcker.

83 **"as reflected in the gold price..."** "Historical Gold Charts," Kitco, https://www.kitco.com/charts/historicalgold.html.

83 **"By 1982, the gold price had fallen..."** "Historical Gold Charts," Kitco, https://www.kitco.com/charts/historicalgold.html.

83 **"Interest rates went way up above our expectations..."** Paul Volcker, interview by Steve Forbes, May 10, 2018, raw transcript interview for *In Money We Trust?* documentary, produced by Our Town Films and BOLDE Communications, distributed by Maryland Public Television, May 10, 2018, film and additional video can be found at https://inmoneywetrust.org/.

83 **"Unemployment [...] exceeded the high of the 2008-09 economic crisis..."** US Bureau of Labor Statistics, "Unemployment Rate," Federal Reserve Bank of St. Louis (FRED), https://fred.stlouisfed.org/series/UNRATE.

83 **"Farmers, who drove their tractors..."** Bill Medley, "Volcker's Announcement of Anti-Inflation Measures," Federal Reserve Bank of St. Louis, October 1979, https://www.federalreservehistory.org/essays/anti-inflation-measures.

84 **"Mexico let it be known that it might default..."** James Boughton, "The Mexican Crisis: No Mountain Too High?" *Silent Revolution: the International Monetary Fund, 1979-1989*, (Washington, DC: International Monetary Fund, 2001), 281.

84 **"the US economy grew by 4.3 percent per year..."** " Percent Change From Preceding Period in Real Gross Domestic Product," Bureau of Economic Analysis, October 28, 2021, https://bit.ly/3wssZ4g.

84 **"The Misery Index..."** Clay Halton, "The Misery Index," Investopedia, June 1, 2021, https://www.investopedia.com/terms/m/miseryindex.asp#citation-4.

84 **"dropped from 22 percent..."** "U.S. Misery Index 1948–The Present," InflationData, https://inflationdata.com/articles/wp-content/uploads/2021/09/Misery-Index2-Aug-2021.png.

84 **"The dollar still fluctuated wildly..."** Kitco, "Historical Gold Charts."

84 **"Alan Greenspan succeeded Volcker as Fed Chair in 1987..."** Board of Governors of the Federal Reserve System, "Alan Greenspan," Federal Reserve Bank of St. Louis, https://www.federalreservehistory.org/people/alan-greenspan.

85 **"He explained in a 2004 Congressional testimony..."** Alan

Greenspan, "Monetary Policy and the State of the Economy," testimony before US House of Representatives, Committee on Financial Services, July 21, 2004, http://commdocs.house.gov/committees/bank/hba96942.000/hba96942_0f.htm.

85 **"Since the late '70s..."** Nathan Lewis, "If Alan Greenspan Wants To 'End the Fed,' Times Must Be Changing," *Forbes*, March 14, 2013.

85 **"The Great Moderation," the low-inflation, high-growth era..."** Craig Hakkio, "The Great Moderation 1982 -2007," Federal Reserve Bank of St. Louis, https://www.federalreservehistory.org/essays/great-moderation.

86 **"A long list of taxes was lowered or discarded..."** Nathan Lewis, "The Flat Tax in Russia," New World Economics, May 30, 2010, https://newworldeconomics.com/the-flat-tax-in-russia/.

86 **"In 2000, he passed a radical 13 percent flat income tax..."** Alvin Rabushka, "The Flat Tax at Work in Russia," *Hoover Daily Report,* February 21, 2002.

86 **"the lowest in the world..."** Daniel Mitchell, "Flat World, Flat Taxes," Cato Institute, April 27, 2007, https://www.cato.org/commentary/flat-world-flat-taxes.

86 **"allowing it to stabilize at around 29 per dollar..."** Lewis, *Gold,* 359.

86 **"the Russian economy grew 10 percent in 2000..."** Lewis, *Gold,* 359.

86 **"interest rates plummeted to less than 10 percent..."** Lewis, "Flat Tax in Russia."

"Interest Rates, Discount Rate for Russian Federation," Federal Reserve Bank of St. Louis (FRED), https://fred.stlouisfed.org/series/INTDSRRUM193N.

87 **"Steve Hanke, who has helped design currency boards..."** Steve Hanke, "Remembrances of a Currency Board Reformer: Some Notes and Sketches from the Field," *Studies in Applied Economics,* No. 55, June 2016.

87 **"a local currency is backed '100 percent'..."** Steve Hanke, interview by Steve Forbes, April 17, 2018, raw transcript interview for *In Money We Trust?* documentary, produced by Our Town Films and BOLDE Communications, distributed by Maryland Public Tele-

vision, December 29, 2018, film and additional video can be found at https://inmoneywetrust.org/.

87  "Two Baltic states..." Andreas Katsis, "Analysis of the Estonian Currency Board," *Studies in Applied Economics*, No. 88, September 2017.

87  "Latvia achieved the same result with a quasi-currency board..." Anders Aslund and Valdis Dombrovskis, "Latvia's Post-Soviet Transition, How Latvia Came Through the Financial Crisis," Peterson Institute for International Economics, May 2011, 9, https://www.piie.com/publications/chapters_preview/6024/01iie6024.pdf.

87  "A number of countries in Africa also use currency board-like systems..." Spencer Abrohms and Kurt Schuler, "A Balance Sheet Analysis of the CFA Franc Zone," *Studies in Applied Economics*, No. 143, December 2019, https://sites.krieger.jhu.edu/iae/files/2019/12/A-Balance-Sheet-Analysis-of-the-CFA-Franc-Zone-1.pdf.

87  "Hong Kong has had a currency board..." Katsis, "Analysis."

88  "In 1997, Hanke advised the government of Bulgaria..." Steve Hanke and Todor Tanev, "On Extending the Currency Board Principle in Bulgaria: Long Live the Currency Board," *Studies in Applied Economics*, No. 140, November 2019, https://www.cato.org/sites/cato.org/files/2019-11/On-Extending-the-Currency-Board-Principle-in-Bulgaria-Long-Live-the-Currency-Board.pdf.

88  "an annual rate at one point surpassing 2,000 percent..." Anne-Marie Guide, "The Role of the Currency Board in Bulgaria's Stabilization," *Finance & Development*, Volume 36, Number 3, (September 1999), https://www.imf.org/external/pubs/ft/fandd/1999/09/gulde.htm.

88  "magically the lev [...] interest rates in Bulgaria were in single digits..." Hanke, interview transcript.

88  "Bulgaria's economy [...] was soon growing at a robust rate of nearly 5 percent..." The World Bank, "GDP Growth (annual %) – Bulgaria," https://data.worldbank.org/indicator/NY.GDP.MKTP.KD.ZG?locations=BG.

88  "there has never been one that has failed..." Hanke, interview transcript.

88  "Argentina set up a 'convertibility system'..." Steve Hanke, "Why Argentina Did Not Have a Currency Board," *Central Banking*, Vol. 8, No. 3, (February 2008), https://www.cato.org/sites/cato.org/files/articles/hanke_feb2008_argentina_currencyboard.pdf.

88    **"Stability might not be everything..."** Hanke, interview transcript.

89    **"no inflation during the gold standard era in the late nineteenth century..."** James Dorn, "How the Classical Gold Standard Can Inform Monetary Policy," *Cato Journal,* Fall 2020.

90    **"In the words of economist Judy Shelton..."** Judy Shelton, interview by Steve Forbes, April 18, 2018, raw transcript interview for *In Money We Trust?* documentary, produced by Our Town Films and BOLDE Communications, distributed by Maryland Public Television, December 29, 2018, film and additional video can be found at https://inmoneywetrust.org/.

92    **"a range of 1 percent, the rate used under the Bretton Woods system..."** Federal Reserve Bank of St. Louis, "Creation of the Bretton Woods System," July 1944, https://www.federalreserve-history.org/essays/bretton-woods-created.

94    **"the United States has only about 261 million ounces of gold..."** United States Treasury, "U.S Treasury Owned Gold," Fiscal Data, https://fiscaldata.treasury.gov/datasets/status-report-government-gold-reserve/u-s-treasury-owned-gold.

94    **"The monetary base is more than $6 trillion..."** Board of Governors of the Federal Reserve System, "Monetary Base; Total," Federal Reserve Bank of St. Louis (FRED), https://fred.stlouisfed.org/series/BOGMBASE.

95    **"Between 1934..."** Douglas Irwin, "Gold Sterilization and the Recession of 1937-38," Working Paper 17595, National Bureau of Economic Research, 12, https://www.nber.org/system/files/working_papers/w17595/w17595.pdf

95    **"and 1971..."** Board of Governors of the Federal Reserve System, "Monetary Base; Total," Federal Reserve Bank of St. Louis, https://fred.stlouisfed.org/series/BOGMBASE.

95    **"while the dollar was fixed to gold at the rate of $35 an ounce..."** "Brief History of the Gold Standard in the United States," Congressional Research Service, June 23, 2011, https://crsreports.congress.gov/product/pdf/R/R41887/2.

95    **"The most pointed charge leveled against gold..."** Barry Eichengreen, *Golden Fetters: The Gold Standard and the Great Depression, 1919-1939* (New York: Oxford University Press, 1992), Introduction.

95    **"The real cause of the beginning of the Great Depression..."** Lewis, *Gold,* 226.

96 **"In 1932, the US enacted a huge tax increase…"** Alan Reynolds, "The Economic Impact of Tax Changes, 1920–1939," *Cato Journal,* Cato Institute, Winter 2021.

96 **"At least twenty countries weakened their currencies…"** Nathan Lewis, "Currency Devaluations of the 1930s," New World Economics, September 30, 2012, https://newworldeconomics.com/ currency-devaluations-of-the-1930s/.

96 **"In 1944, allies and neutral nations convened in New Hampshire…"** Sandra Kollen Ghizoni, "Creation of the Bretton Woods System July 1944," Federal Reserve Bank of St. Louis, https://www. federalreservehistory.org/essays/bretton-woods-created.

CHAPTER FIVE:
WHAT ABOUT YOUR MONEY?

97 **"*Forbes* magazine featured…"** "Inflation: You Are Losing Your Assets," *Forbes,* April 1, 1974, 28.

98 **"the inflation-adjusted Dow Jones Industrial Average fell…"** "Dow Jones - DJIA - 100 Year Historical Chart," Macrotrends, https://www.macrotrends.net/1319/dow-jones-100-year-historical-chart.

98 **"the first decade of the twenty-first century…"** "Dow Jones - DJIA - 100 Year Historical Chart," Macrotrends, https://www.macrotrends.net/1319/dow-jones-100-year-historical-chart.

99 **"The methodology [ … ] has changed…"** US Bureau of Labor Statistics, "Consumer Price Index," https://www.bls.gov/cpi/additional-resources/historical-changes.htm.

99 **"different versions of the CPI…"** Barclay Palmer, "Why Is the Consumer Price Index Controversial?" Investopedia, July 23, 2021, https://www.investopedia.com/articles/07/consumerpriceindex.asp.

99 **"The CPI Inflation Calculator…"** US Bureau of Labor Statistics, https://www.bls.gov/data/inflation_calculator.htm.

99 **"the PCE is an index of prices…"** Bureau of Economic Analysis, "The Personal Consumption Expenditure Price Index," https://www. bea.gov/data/personal-consumption-expenditures-price-index

99 **"Unlike the CPI…"** Noah Johnson, "A comparison of PCE and CPI: Methodological Differences in U.S. Inflation Calculation and their Implications," research paper, US Bureau of Labor Statistics,

November 2017, https://www.bls.gov/osmr/research-papers/2017/pdf/stl70010.pdf.

100 **"the annual inflation level in July of 2020..."** BLS Data Viewer, US Bureau of Labor Statistics, https://beta.bls.gov/dataViewer/view/timeseries/CUUR0000SA0.

101 **"In 2021, rising oil prices..."** US Energy Information Administration, "Petroleum & Other Liquids," chart, https://www.eia.gov/dnav/pet/hist/RWTCD.htm.

101 **"Biden administration's new restrictions..."** Ben Cahill, "Biden Makes Sweeping Changes to Oil and Gas Policy," Center for Strategic & International Studies, January 28, 2021, https://www.csis.org/analysis/biden-makes-sweeping-changes-oil-and-gas-policy.

102 **"The central bank's assets and liabilities are published..."** "Factors Affecting Reserve Balances – H.4.1," Federal Reserve, https://www.federalreserve.gov/releases/h41/.

102 **"Where to Get Money Supply Information..."** Federal Reserve, "Money Stock Measures–H.6 Release," https://www.federalreserve.gov/releases/h6/current/default.htm.

103 **"the velocity of money..."** Federal Reserve Bank of St. Louis, "Velocity of M2 Money Stock," Federal Reserve Bank of St. Louis (FRED), https://fred.stlouisfed.org/series/M2V.

106 **"between 1969 and 1980, the price of oil..."** Federal Reserve Bank of St, Louis, "Spot Crude Oil Price: West Texas Intermediate (WTI)," Federal Reserve Bank of St. Louis (FRED), https://fred.stlouisfed.org/series/WTISPLC.

106 **"stock price of oil giant Exxon..."** "ExxonMobil Corporation," Yahoo!Finance, 2021, https://finance.yahoo.com/quote/XOM/history?period1=-31536000&period2=340156800&interval=1d&filter=history&frequency=1d&includeAdjustedClose=true.

106 **"Neither investment performed well..."** "When Exxon Could Have Beaten Intel," *Forbes*, July 7, 1997.

107 **"A Zilog senior executive..."** "Oral History Panel on the Development and Promotion of the Zilog Z8000 Microprocessor," (transcript) Computer History Museum Archive, April 27, 2007, https://archive.computerhistory.org/resources/access/text/2015/06/102658075-05-01-acc.pdf.

107 **"Warren Buffett has pointed out..."** Warren Buffett address

to Berkshire Hathaway shareholders, Berkshire Hathaway, February 27, 1981, https://www.berkshirehathaway.com/letters/1980.html.

108  **"annual list of 'Dividend Aristocrats'..."** John Divine, "2021 Dividend Aristocrats List: All 65 Stocks," *US News & World Report*, May 7, 2021.

110  **"annual returns of more than 9 percent..."** James Royal, PhD, Arielle O'Shea, "What is the Average Stock Market Return?" NerdWallet, August 11, 2021, https://www.nerdwallet.com/article/investing/average-stock-market-return.

110  **"A SPAC is a speculative device..."** "What You Need To Know About SPACs," US Securities and Exchange Commission, May 25, 2021, https://www.sec.gov/oiea/investor-alerts-and-bulletins/what-you-need-know-about-spacs-investor-bulletin.

111  **"Some Tips About TIPS..."** Brian O'Connell and John Schmidt, "Treasury Inflation-Protected Securities (TIPS)," *Forbes*, April 13, 2021.

112  **"During the 1970s, US housing prices rose 148%..."** US Census Bureau and US Department of Housing and Urban Development, "Average Sales Price of Houses Sold for the United States," Federal Reserve Bank of St. Louis (FRED), https://fred.stlouisfed.org/series/ASPUS.

112  **"three biggest homebuilding booms..."** US Census Bureau and US Department of Housing and Urban Development, "New Privately-Owned Housing Units Started: Total Units," Federal Reserve Bank of St. Louis (FRED), https://fred.stlouisfed.org/series/HOUST.

113  **"desperate New York City landlords..."** Valeria Ricciuilli, "In the 1970s, the Bronx was Burning, but Some Residents Were Rebuilding," Curbed New York, May 3, 2019, https://ny.curbed.com/2019/5/3/18525908/south-bronx-fires-decade-of-fire-vivian-vazquez-documentary.

114  **"their yields were near 8 percent..."** Historical REIT Spreads: Dividend Yields vs. U.S. Treasuries," Millionacres, updated August 10, 2021, https://www.millionacres.com/real-estate-investing/reits/reit-investing-101/historical-reit-spreads-divi-dend-yields-vs-us-treasuries/.

114  **"yields on REITs have hovered between 2 and 3 percent..."** Lisa Springer, "10 Best REITs for the Rest of 2021," Kiplinger, August 31, 2021, https://www.kiplinger.com/investing/reits/603383/10-best-reits-for-the-rest-of-2021.

114 **"Exchange Traded Funds consisting of REITs..."** Investopedia, "REITs vs. REIT ETFs: How They Compare," May 16, 2021, https://www.investopedia.com/articles/investing/081415/reits-vs-reit-etfs-how-they-compare.asp.

114 **"Timber REITs..."** Matthew Frankel, "How to Invest in Timber REITs," Motley Fool, August 27, 2019, https://www.fool.com/investing/how-to-invest-in-timber-reits.aspx.

114 **"US farmland REITs..."** Matthew DiLallo, "Investing in Farmland: A Real Estate Investor's Guide," Millionacres, October 4, 2021, https://www.millionacres.com/real-estate-investing/investing-farmland-real-estate-investors-guide/.

115 **"in the late 1960s, gold was priced at $35 an ounce..."** "Historical Gold Charts," Kitco, https://www.kitco.com/charts/historical-gold.html.

116 **"an ounce of gold was roughly worth sixteen ounces of silver..."** Larry Margasak, "Silver vs. Gold: William Steinway's Wedge Issue of the 1896 Election," National Museum of American History, October 29, 2014, https://americanhistory.si.edu/blog/silver-vs-gold-william-steinways-wedge-issue-1896-election.

116 **"more than seventy ounces of silver..."** APMEX, "Precious Metal Sizes Conversion Chart," https://www.apmex.com/education/science/oz-to-gram-to-kilo-to-grain-conversion-tables.

116 **"its value versus gold falls to historical lows, as it did in 2020..."** Longtermtrends, "Gold to Silver Ratio," https://www.longtermtrends.net/gold-silver-ratio/.

117 **"tech visionaries like Elon Musk..."** Billy Bambrough, "Tesla Billionaire Elon Musk Signals Surprise Dogecoin 'Update' Support as The Bitcoin Price Suddenly Surges," *Forbes*, October 14, 2021.

117 **"Companies like Musk's Tesla..."** Noor Zainab Hussain and Nivedita Balu, "Tesla Will 'Most Likely' Restart Accepting Bitcoin as Payments, Says Musk," Reuters, July 22, 2021, https://www.reuters.com/business/autos-transportation/tesla-will-most-likely-restart-accepting-bitcoin-payments-says-musk-2021-07-21/.

117 **"and also PayPal..."** PayPal Developer, "Cryptocurrency at PayPal," https://developer.paypal.com/docs/crypto/.

117 **"El Salvador [...] making Bitcoin legal tender..."** Wilfredo Pineda and Nelson Renteria, "One Month On, El Salvador's Bitcoin Use Grows but Headaches Persist," Reuters, October 8, 2021,

https://www.reuters.com/technology/one-month-el-salvadors-bitcoin-use-grows-headaches-persist-2021-10-07/.

118 **"Bitcoin [...] lose half its value in a single day..."** Charles Bovaird, "Bitcoin Lost Roughly 50% Of Its Value in A Day," *Forbes*, March 12, 2020.

118 **"A new class of cryptocurrencies [...] "stablecoins"..."** Adam Hayes, "Stablecoin," Investopedia, updated October 8, 2021, https://www.investopedia.com/terms/s/stablecoin.asp.

118 **"growing concerns that these cryptos..."** Andy Kessler, "Crypto is Shedding its Tether," *Wall Street Journal*, October 24, 2021.

119 **"a wrenching deflation that saw the price of oil collapse..."** Federal Reserve Bank of St. Louis, "Spot Crude Oil Price: West Texas Intermediate (WTI)", Federal Reserve Bank of St. Louis (FRED), https://fred.stlouisfed.org/series/WTISPLC.

119 **"After Ronald Reagan was elected..."** "Historical Gold Charts," Kitco, https://www.kitco.com/charts/historicalgold.html.

121 **"Between 1950 and 1970, Japan's GDP..."** Nathan Lewis, "Greece Needs the Magic Formula to Become the Wealthiest Country in the Eurozone," New World Economics, March 26, 2015, https://newworldeconomics.com/greece-needs-the-magic-formula-to-become-the-wealthiest-country-in-the-eurozone/.

121 **"Soviet Union [...] falling apart into fifteen nations in 1991..."** John Dewdney, "Soviet Union," *Encyclopedia Britannica*, https://www.britannica.com/place/Soviet-Union.

121 **"'Flat tax' income-tax systems adopted..."** Daniel Mitchell, "Flat World, Flat Taxes," Cato Institute, April 27, 2007, https://www.cato.org/commentary/flat-world-flat-taxes.

121 **"growth rates of flat tax-adopting countries..."** Nathan Lewis, "Rise of the Flat Tax Gives Us Morning in Albania," *Forbes*, September 29, 2011.

## CHAPTER SIX:
## THE WAY FORWARD

123 **"minting a $1 trillion coin..."** Judy Shelton, "How the Fed Finances U.S. Debt," *Wall Street Journal*, October 13, 2021.

124 **"address issues like 'climate change'..."** Lael Brainard, "Finan-

cial Stability Implications of Climate Change," Federal Reserve, March 23, 2021, https://www.federalreserve.gov/newsevents/speech/brainard20210323a.htm.

Alexander William Salter and Daniel Smith, "End the Fed's Mission Creep," *Wall Street Journal*, March 25, 2021.

125 **"In the words of *Newsweek*..."** Josh Hammer, "COVID-19 Has Forever Destroyed Americans' Trust in Ruling Class 'Experts,'" *Newsweek*, June 4, 2021.

126 **"330 million people..."** US Census Bureau, "U.S. and World Population Clock," https://www.census.gov/popclock/.

128 **"per capita income would be 72 percent higher..."** Bureau of Economic Analysis, "Table 7.1 Selected Per Capita Product and Income Series in Current and Chained Dollars," https://apps.bea.gov/iTable/index_nipa.cfm.

129 **"economy would be at least 50 percent bigger..."** Bureau of Economic Analysis, "Table 1.1.1 Percent Change from Preceding Period in Real Gross Domestic Product," https://apps.bea.gov/iTable/index_nipa.cfm.

Bureau of Economic Analysis, "Table 1.1.6 Real Gross Domestic Product, Chained Dollars," https://apps.bea.gov/iTable/index_nipa.cfm.

130 **"John Locke called inflation..."** Felix Waldmann, "Additions to De Beer's Correspondence of John Locke," *Locke Studies*, 15, February 2018, 31-52, https://ojs.lib.uwo.ca/index.php/locke/article/view/672/444.

130 **"Keynes famously observed..."** John Maynard Keynes, *The Economic Consequences of the Peace* (New York: Harcourt, Brace, and Howe: 1920).

131 **"According to one study, their frequency has doubled since the early 1970s..."** Michael Bordo, Barry Eichengreen, Daniela Klingebiel, Maria Soledad Martinez-Peria and Andrew Rose, "Is the Crisis Problem Growing More Severe?" *Economic Policy*, 32:51-82.

132 **"more wealth was created during that century..."** Angus Maddison, "World Per Capita GDP (Inflation Adjusted)" (chart) *The World Economy: A Millennial Perspective*, (OECD, 2001) 264.

132 **"and also the decade of the 1960s..."** US Bureau of Labor Statistics, "Unemployment Rate," Federal Reserve Bank of St. Louis (FRED), https://fred.stlouisfed.org/series/UNRATE.

# Index